Other Lives
Our Own

Jason Weiss

S P U Y T E N   D U Y V I L
New York City

Acknowledgments

The author would like to thank the following publications where some of these texts first appeared: *Airplane Reading* (2023), "Skyward"; *Open Doors Review* (2023), "Transient Light"; *Tinta Regada* (2024), "Potocki," "*La Habanera*," "Meadowland"; *Le Ventre et l'Oreille* (2023), "Canary"; *Brooklyn Non Fiction* (2023), "Propelled by a Stranger to Unexpected Delights"; *Beach Badge* (2024), "Rooms."

Special thanks to Norton Wisdom for permission to reproduce his painting on the cover, "Mermaid Kiss" (inspired by an Oscar Wilde story).

Library of Congress Control Number: 2024952383

CONTENTS

UNWAY

Unway. Behind me, I began to realize what I was hearing. Unway. Unway. Punctuating by some mysterious rhythm the excited commentary of two eleven-year-old girls from Lyon on their first visit to Brooklyn, the two syllables were not French. I was driving the car—unway—and no sooner did I reach the corner than I saw what they were saying. They were making a game of spotting the One Way street signs as we drove along. Unway. Unway. Because it did not make immediate sense to my ears, I did not dwell on it. And then, it was kind of cute the way the girls mispronounced the word. Unway. I didn't want to correct them, never did all that weekend. They were supposed to be practicing their English, but I spoke their language more with them. They would have plenty of opportunity over the next four weeks—they were on their way to an international camp upstate, where the default language was English, and we were their volunteer hosts for the first weekend. It had never occurred to me to pronounce *won* way as unway. That granted a whole new perspective—but only to me, since they knew what they meant, even if their pronunciation was mistaken. From where I sat, I understood; and understood again, added value. Unway.

WHERE ARE YOU FROM

The question asks too much and not enough. What carried you the whole long way up to now? It encapsulates your entire life before today. What godforsaken place sent you forth, that you had to leave for your own good? The immigrant's greeting; the nativist's scorn. You would seem to be from somewhere else. But so are most people.

Where are you from? The answer is never really complete, no matter how much you go on. Is anyone listening past the first sentence? Lie all you want, make a performance of it, yank at the heartstrings like a double bassist. Who's to know if the facts are taking a vacation? Your accent; the way you dress; something you do or say sounds not quite right. Benefit of the doubt: of course, you're a stranger. Then perhaps it would be helpful to explain, why are you here? Not that anyone should have to give a reason.

Where are you from? The response matters less than the assertion, in the form of an interrogation, that you are probably not one of us. And yet, how can we help but inquire, as though we'd wandered into a fabulous bazaar. Almost certainly you brought something with you from wherever that was, something we don't have and were perhaps unaware of. Rest assured, your contribution (local color, at least) will be expected. Thus, the accounting: to take stock of the ingredients that surely went into you, with all their enchantment and drama.

We can only be in one place at a time, physically. A subway car on the B train that has just emerged onto the bridge toward Chinatown. And before you rode through those dark tunnels? It is indiscreet to ask where you are from. Our human dignity demands that we treat everyone the same, as we would ourselves be treated. Less than that is unacceptable. Still, we yearn for the epic sweep, to be witnesses (preferably at a safe distance), to hear directly from the mouth of one who may have suffered. We want to be reassured of our good fortune in remaining where we are. Think of how much worse others have it, had it, will have it. For the rest of us, we attempt to build the past from the present, even if sometimes out of distraction we slip up in posing that intimate question. Tell us stories, we ask, of the places that were yours, that seemed like they would go on forever, just as we in turn recount our own. Where are you from? All those places that existed for a time, so many more than today.

But does it matter where anyone is from? If we are here on this corner now, in this room, this neighborhood, this town, what difference does it make how we each threaded our way? In whatever measure we forge our own destiny, there is nonetheless a gap, an interval of chance, of the unpredictable, that swings us along as we swing with it. Most often I will not ask, out of shyness and discretion, but I am always curious regarding those I happen to encounter. I want to know something about the face, the eyes before me, a little is a lot, enough to dream, to go where I have never been.

Learning Whiteness

More than a vast exercise in foolishness, or a monumental hoax played on the world, the myth of whiteness turned out to be a ludicrous practice of self-deception, risen from a desperate Europe and an anxious America.

But right from the start, in any consciousness of itself, America had to know better. Europe too, of course: soon as you cross a river or a mountain, let alone a sea, and partake of another people's water and the fruits of their land, from then on their welfare is also your concern. And America, which was first of all a story of stolen land, was from its earliest development a grand experiment in *mixages*, a forced jumbling of peoples from everywhere. So, whiteness was less a factor for claiming a coherent identity than it was an economic tool for maintaining dominance.

At the same time, it's well known that whiteness can cause blindness. The glare, as light bounces across your eyes; or an interminable fog of whiteness that swallows you up. If all you see is white, then you've seen nothing. Who taught us to look in that way?

When I was growing up in the 1960s, in a town on

the Jersey shore halfway between Long Branch and Asbury Park, I lived in a mostly white world. As a child, being Jewish, I was aware of who else was Jewish and who was not. Eventually, I had classmates with Irish names, and German, Italian, Czech, British. As for who belonged to what church, I didn't understand any of that. Besides, the orthodox synagogue on Asbury Avenue that we attended (now a Haitian Baptist church, building unchanged), I don't think any of my local Jewish friends went there. Compounding that divide, up through my middle school years, I mostly went to a Hebrew day school a few towns over, in Wanamassa, but I rebelled and left twice and graduated from the local public school. So, already I didn't feel quite the same as anyone around me, and if someone had tried to explain, But you're all white, that wouldn't have made any sense to me.

White people, I came to realize, were an illusion. If that was what we had in common, it wasn't much. And who knows if it was true? Identity by default; the *we* are not *them* crowd. Not black, not brown, not any people of color do we come from (far as we know), what's left? When I was a child, no one talked explicitly about being white, it just seemed to be the norm. What a twisted world, in retrospect. I understood, Jews were not going to be the norm. Who were these white people and what was so special about them?

Five Strings

Maybe Isaac suggested the idea. Or probably it was Nicky, since he lived there in DF. I knew about *peñas* and was eager to go to one. I had heard about their popularity in Chile and Argentina, as the breeding ground for the new Latin American song movement—but I don't think I was aware before that they also existed in Mexico. Must have been Nicky said I should bring my banjo.

Way back in the summer of '73, I was seventeen, Isaac was eighteen, and we were driving from southern California all the way down and across through Mexico in his Chevy van (fixed up for sleeping), and further south into Guatemala and back. A good two months we were on the road. I had never been to Mexico beyond a quick visit to Baja with him, but he had grown up in Tijuana as well as the California side. We stuck around a bit in Mexico City each way, so that's how Nicky, his cousin, joined us for half our epic journey. And as we traveled, sometimes I took out my banjo to play, even attracting a small audience. The idea of performing a few tunes in a *peña*, though, seemed a special privilege.

Certainly, the banjo was an incongruous creature up on that coffee house stage, or anywhere else in Mexico.

I didn't much dwell on that distinction at the time. The instrument was quintessentially American, meaning the United States, and before that, it was African. If its aspect, its sound, did not exactly stir up images of gringo spies and operatives, its folksy implications suggested at minimum a naïf from foreign lands. With my long hair and scraggly beard, I was more a Berkeley bumpkin; in any case, I looked not unlike people who were seated before me. I had been fascinated with American traditional music but was lately drifting away from that toward something else, so whether the listeners had a clue what to expect on seeing the banjo, they didn't really. I launched into a winding instrumental piece of my own making, with an odd shape and odd scales, Eastern sounding, sort of modal. However it sprang into my head, I was very fond of that tune. The audience seemed to like it too. All the same, in closing I gave them what the instrument itself had promised in a way, something from the tradition, an old song. "Oh, Susanna," by way of James Taylor's version. Unless, it might have been "The Cuckoo" I played.

Uncanny Resemblance

We should be able to recognize the person we were forty years ago. Even if, as some say, they have no desire to meet that person. Grown from an individual who should have known better perhaps; but also growth away, movement.

We are not trees, are we? Moving targets; not where we were. So, to know ourselves seems to mandate a moving perspective, here and there. All the things we would tell that person if encountered by chance, that person we were long ago; most of it unimportant. Startled we are, time and again, to survive so much movement. Anyhow, who was that stranger, that phantom from the past? And why were they looking at us? What do they think we know?

Spirit of the Letter

The sense of how, on speaking a foreign language (one learned after childhood), we sometimes end up like actors when we speak. Though I never adopted the Castilian "s" sound, even when in Ethpanya, I have often taken on the *porteño* pronunciation of the "y" sound as *zh. Zho soy...* But I am not altogether consistent in that affectation either. What to make of a personality who cannot even be relied on to speak always with the same accent? For me, it is just the result of having learned Spanish in California plus travels in Mexico. There the elyay (the name of the letter *ll*, the sound of which by a translingual pun could be thought to mean "praise god") is simply the "y" as in youth. Hearing it as *zh* in the speech of Argentine friends, I have tended to make a semi-conscious adjustment to speak closer to the way they do. It's true I don't do this with other regional speech patterns in Spanish or French; and maybe it's been only a year I've tended to really adopt that habit with Argentines, since I first visited Buenos Aires.

What do we call that—an adaptation to the environment? Seeking to be a little less foreign to each other, and yet. As a non-native speaker, I take my cue from others who know. And what settles the usage in my ear is to hear it in people's names—three Guillermos I've become friends with, and one Guillermina, just in the past year. But when I'm not quite thinking about it sometimes I revert to the *ll* I heard first, can't be helped. Still, that shift to the Argentine way must surely be a reflex of sympathy, and at the same time it marks a sort of wobble, a slight uncertainty, in my identity as a speaker of Spanish. In learning another language or more, it seems, no one can say who my parents are; I have many.

Mirror, Mirror

The person in front of the mirror says, "That's not me. Someone else is looking back." It cannot be easy, day after day, to know an impostor wears your face, speaks with your voice, carries you prisoner inside. To arrive at that conviction seems remarkable enough; more than just a feeling, a nagging discomfort, what grows into a kind of certainty implies an internal trajectory along which no return is possible. What provoked the awakening? It must have long been stirring in the depths. Yet another instance where a newfound consciousness might hardly be a blessing, for the difficulties it now makes visible. At the same time, how many people really achieve an understanding of who they are, even by way of determining who they are not? But the mask, if it be so recognized, does not yield readily. Everyone is used to it and thinks it is you, just as their own masks hang firmly in place, imperceptible to them, having never wavered or given cause to wonder.

The face we present to the world does not announce its latent treachery. As the bearers of that face, we don't quite know how to see it. Others are our mirror, as we to them; except, it is rather a shattered mirror, each shard tossing back another view of us through time. A composite image, impossible to read. Besides, when we look at other people, we notice what their faces tell of them, not how it reflects our own (nightmarish thought: a brain condition where we could not see anyone's face for itself, as of another person, but only as a reflection of ourselves, with all its subjectivity intact). Whatever we do perceive there remains subliminal or bobbing at the surface of our waking minds. Before us, a vague if familiar apparition speaking in mysteries.

Our face in the mirror, it turns out, is already not our own anymore. Gone off to roam the world without us somehow. Who we are does not choose the face that is ours, the one that is still there when we're not looking. Inner forces shape that face, as much as the sun and the rain; as much as the ground that sent us forth.

Skyward

What could be more peculiar than flying in an airplane? No matter how many hundreds of times we've joined the procession to file into that big metal tube, no matter how used to it we may be, the experience remains utterly unnatural. We may feign nonchalance, seasoned veterans of flight, but if the gods had wanted us to be able to propel ourselves through the air, would we not have been born with a jetpack strapped securely to our back, probably in green or blue? Or, let us suppose that the careless gods merely figured we might find a way, sooner or later, to fill in the blanks. Or some of the blanks, for we are barely a hundred years into this flight thing. There we are, then, seated on a plane smiling at the person next to us, elbows tucked carefully into our sides. We might even tumble into a long and unexpected conversation with them, surprised at our own affability or downright candidness, at the end of which we will still not know their name, despite having been treated to photos of the new grandchild. So much do we take for granted this mode of transport that we no longer bother to remind ourselves that air travel is statistically far safer than by car. Seems counterintuitive, but on the other hand we'd prefer not to know if the facts proved otherwise.

Self-preservation tells us that when standing on a ledge—or way up on a tightrope pausing in the yawning gap between why and why not—we would do best to not look down. That vertigo induced by the recognition of our own folly. So, how come a mere sheet of glass is enough for us to relinquish such advice as we gaze wonderingly upon the clouds beneath us? Do we really think they will catch us if we fall? And how is it that the movie we are watching, from our perch in the airborne drive-in that goes hurtling through space, doesn't disintegrate before we ever glimpse a single spark? Locomotion, indeed; very loco.

In our suspended animation between one location and the next, that fluid and incessant nowhere which lays claim to us as if we shall never know another place, as if the going were our sole condition and habitation a deluded dream, we cling nonetheless to the thought that there is a place (if not several) where we are really we. The place seems to define us and not all that lies in between there and every destination. Up in the air, within that pressurized cabin, our present existence could not be more elusive. How do we keep up the momentum of faith that we ourselves will arrive not just in one piece but as much one integrated person as when we left wherever that was, whoever we were?

These paradoxes of flight should change us in some way each time we launch forth; even to a small degree, on a molecular level perhaps. Alice was not unaffected when she stepped through the looking glass. In the scientific realm, albeit a more extreme circumstance, it was recently discovered that the astronaut Scott Kelly returned to Earth with his very DNA altered after an extended stay in outer space. Air travel within our planet's atmosphere, regardless how routine the trajectory, might well yield subtler internal shifts. Nor would first-class passengers be exempt from the pull of otherworldly forces: coddled in their ample cocoons, would they not be the first to grow horns, their bodies expanding with new appendages in spaces that can fit them?

STUCK DOWN A LONG DIRT ROAD

The situation in this country has grown so dire that to say we live in a civilized society can only be understood as an aspiration, in a future that continues to escape us. So, I don't hesitate, in recent years, when I'm visiting with foreign-born friends who live outside the US, to regale them with stories about the costs of education and healthcare in America. If nothing else, they can consider themselves lucky in that respect; while I settle for the morbid amusement of watching their jaws drop.

Once I have imparted such information to my friends, we have little left to say on the matter since we all share the same astonishment. What society does that to itself? Might as well shoot yourself in the leg, the arm, the head. Are there countries more brutal in their education and health policies? What ends are served by perpetuating such blindness? Well do we know the interests who profit; still, it seems quite mind-boggling how a society could allow the wretched state of affairs to fester as it has, courting the possibility of collapse. To achieve a system, as a principle of our self-government, where education and healthcare are guaranteed for everyone is almost inconceivable in America, just as the absence of those assurances is inconceivable in most other countries. Exceptionalism, indeed. Freedom to perish from crushing debt. Freedom to be skinned alive by every charlatan and biblethumper.

To see one's country as a bad example among nations. Not for the sake of illusions about other lands; but rather, in trying to be realistic about a history of wrong choices we might yet hope to learn from. I began to imagine that every non-American knew more about American crimes than Americans did. I still don't know if I am mistaken in that assumption. As Americans, we have a responsibility at least to be a little aware of what goes on around the world in our names. Or are we not also part of American "interests" so often invoked? Regardless of whether we want to be included, and even though the term has no such inclusion in mind, we are nonetheless implicated. And yet, it all seems quite out of our hands—the actions abroad as much as the policies at home that would deprive us of any real security, or any secure reality. We are born to a country that is afraid of itself (with good reason), and that alienates everyone.

In a way, it doesn't seem right to mock the barbarity of American social policy. Or not right for an American to do the mocking, in the company of non-Americans. In a country so monumentally wealthy, the shame should stop us in our tracks. But how else to bear the craziness, the sickness, if not to laugh at it? A form of singing alone in the dark, as the wind howls about. Or is it the wolves we hear, prowling closer?

Becoming Foreigners

Who are we when we travel abroad? What does where we are from count for if at all? And why, of all places, did we set off in that direction?

Surely we had expectations. Things might be different there, they had to be different. No other reason to bother with the going. If we're lucky, curiosity charts the course: a song, a face. Or we are thrown onto the open road, no choice, keep moving.

In another place, we are always someone else and maybe also the same. A little disoriented, almost lost, unsure of what we know. We speak another tongue, and our own tongue becomes different too: a secret among strangers, possibly a trap. The fact is we are more than what we were, and even a bit less, when we make ourselves into foreigners.

CALLING AHEAD

Those of us who do not fit, do not want to fit in with what most other people seem to do or think (or not think), no doubt we got restless at an early age with *things as they are*. Or: what we were told how things are, how they are presented as being. The child's instinct to question was paramount. Was it science or the dullness of blind faith, the laziness of habit, that determined things were just so? How much were we willing to accept, in the manner of a temporary truce, to keep peace with our elders? Who knows, they might be right, but their fragile authority was not a lot to go on. We couldn't help it, not from mere disobedience, the mind turns and so the eyes wonder. What choice did we have but to be playful with the world? If it was a choice at all.

The same inclinations, to look beyond what is given, often compel us to favor cultural experiences that come from outside our own native horizons. Perhaps it's easier to preserve the mystery of our encounters where we do not know the language so well. What lies normally within our reach—all too familiar, possibly overlooked—claims no urgency; it will always be there (if it ever was). We want to go some distance to get to the experience. It should cost us a little, not too much, the better to prepare us for what we find. Yet always to remember it's a gamble: in spite of our efforts, we might well misunderstand the exchanges we have made, or else be swept away beyond ourselves. And that, of course, may really be what we were seeking.

But this lack of urgency about the familiar, is that a privilege only some of us enjoy? Hardly. We would sooner shy away from the reckoning, for there lies the promise of imminent loss, however long delayed. We do well to hold those we love when possible, to recognize our attachments, even as we stir free. What, then, of the geographies and architectures, the neighbors and acquaintances, that situated us, accompanied us through the unfolding days and years, that we scarcely looked at, or looked without quite seeing, or if we saw, already saw past? They gazed back at us and somehow realized we were gone, if not in that moment then the next. Where we went, the telling tries and tries to mark those absent steps, like birds circling, their songs as perches, calling ahead.

LIGHT BULBS

Somewhere along the way, apparently well before we were born, a set of standards was adopted in almost every practice, trade, and discipline we can imagine. The housing industry, for instance: how many decades or centuries has it been that doors and windows are built in the same sizes? The whole rest of the house depends on those measures. Builders, suppliers, architects take these standards as part of the common language. Such norms are familiar to us in so many details big and small—we notice them only when we go someplace else where the norms are different. Until we get used to those in turn and cease to think about the matter.

The overlap of standards across different lands leaves occasional gaps in perspective, but through the course of time, or at least through our own lifetime, we expect nothing to change. An electrical socket in whatever country, it's always going to be like it is, is it not? Then what about light bulbs? Light bulb sockets have generally not changed much either since the early days, but as for the light bulbs themselves, that's where I stumbled down a hole recently. Who pays attention to these things? You berate yourself for not having been smarter in the moment. Three times I went to the hardware store!

For the past couple decades, we have lived in an old house built at the turn of the previous century. Twenty years before we came along, from what we can tell, several owners back, in the late '70s, renovations from top to bottom gave the house a modern feel inside. Light fixtures with white glass globes that the bulbs lit up, always in multiples. So, the kids' bedroom, which one and then the other had in high school, has an ensemble of three glass globes hanging from the ceiling. When one bulb goes out, you want to replace it with the same tone of light. As the market evolved, from incandescent to compact fluorescent to LED, along with ideas about what is the healthiest kind of light, warm to cool, that affected what you find on the shelves. Without thinking too much, you reach for what makes sense at the time. How difficult can it be? You don't have to look at everything to buy a light bulb.

Except that you do, since there are more choices involved now. Light bulbs are not the easy fit they once seemed to be. The fixture that forty years ago was modern is now vintage and almost alien to the range of light bulbs today. We are encouraged to update old habits: the newer kinds of bulbs, being more energy-efficient, put out more light for less consumption, so where the fixture is marked not to use greater than sixty-watt bulbs, I can now consider even a hundred watts, since those bulbs only consume, in fact, seventeen. Why not opt for more light? Is that not the very mark of civilization, knowledge, progress? But a little knowledge, as we are aware, can be a dangerous thing, or at the very least may trip us up in our haste. Two bulbs out of the three were dead, in the fixture in the kids' bedroom, and the third was a compact fluorescent, which had risen and fallen as the new technology in barely a decade; I had previously gone in circles, a year before, replacing one or another bulb, to make sure they were all the same cooler, white light. As I understood, those were already being phased out—and were also more of a hassle to recycle, as they contain mercury—in favor of the newer LED bulbs. So, there I was at the hardware store ready to replace them all with white, hundred-watt bulbs. The salesman pointed to a couple of shelves, and I just had to decide between the ones that claimed to last thirteen years, also the brightest and most expensive, and the others that were a little less so in all respects, lasting a mere nine years. Either way, the life of such bulbs seemed unreal to me, who's going to remember, though it does mean you better choose well because you'll be married to them; I went for the more expensive bulbs. I noticed only when I got home and took them out of the box that the bulbs were a little fatter, but okay so what. I climbed on the chair, removed one globe, set it down, removed the bulb, screwed in the new bulb, tested it out, great, and went to put the globe back on— only it did not fit over the fatter bulb.

Another related question kept gnawing at me along the way, sending me into a fit of research, without which I could not advance to making the right decision. I had been aware of the question for some time, but the prospect of committing to such long-lasting bulbs reminded me I should try to get better informed so that I might choose well. The cooler, whiter light that I preferred—described technically as bluer—more like daylight, was apparently harder on the eyes; further, using that light at night could likely cause difficulties in falling asleep (never a problem for me). I read various articles on the internet, and even passed by to ask my optometrist, who was not in and his assistants had no idea; the fellow at the hardware store was stumped too and could only conclude it depended on individual taste. How was I to worry about the healthier choice when no one seemed to agree?

A couple days later, I returned to the store and found on the same shelves another type of LED bulb shaped like a stick, surely those would fit. I had already concluded, using another of the fatter bulbs in a fixture over the bath that also served as a night light, that a hundred watts was too bright (let alone three times that in the bedroom fixture), meaning I knew even better now what I wanted; I had also brought one of the glass globes to make sure the bulb would fit inside it. Back home, however, I saw that the bulb-stick was too long for the bathroom fixture, so I drove over to the store yet again, that same day. I had surely entered the realm of the ridiculous with these bulbs and I intended to get it resolved. Next to the other bulbs I noticed another box that somehow I hadn't seen before, which said these LED bulbs were normal size: the obvious solution to my problem, new tech in old shape. Why I hadn't noticed them in the first place I still can't fathom.

A Circuitous Account
of His Classroom Years

Surely it must be part of the process to feel at odds with your schooling. Just ask most anyone who's endured some measure of religious education, sooner or later they'll throw an egg, a petard, even a bomb, at the esteemed edifice scowling down at them. Squaring off like that can have lifelong benefits, and usually does, but the realm of secular instruction exerts a push and pull of comparable persuasion, if not more so. The purpose of schooling, after all, beyond imparting knowledge and encouraging just enough spirit of inquiry to move things along (but not too much), is to bring into the fold, lest the young charges go too early astray. As children, we follow along more or less willingly, aware that we haven't much choice in the matter; besides, don't we want to equip ourselves to join the world of our parents and other adults? Never mind that with each day, each month, in the long years of our childhood, we grow ever more convinced of what a mess that world is. And never mind that many among us do not recognize ourselves in what is taught, as we try on one ill-fitting mask after another. In some small measure, it is reassuring to see where we don't fit, that we cannot be so easily swallowed up into the fold.

Often enough, of course, the mind struggles to catch up with what is felt. And there are all sorts of circumstances to show why the institutions we are wedded to through our classroom years are not the best match for our well-being. Or, always possible, some of us cannot help but nurture the mysterious disposition within ourselves that refuses, time and again, to play along with the plan laid out for us. Our trust, in a word, is not so readily earned by the establishment in question. On my very first day at Hillel School, it was clear (at least in retrospect) that I was one of those children. Settled into my kindergarten class, I noticed through the doorway my older brother leaving the building. What was going on? No sooner did I happily embark on my new adventure, I was being abandoned there. Seeing how upset I was, the teacher had to explain that my brother was simply going out with the rest of his class for recess. An incident of practically no significance except that I remember it: first sign, perhaps, that school was meant to trick me.

I always had limited patience with the formalities and presumptions of school, at every stage. In the doctrinal sense, I tended to be wary of joining the club. Beyond that, I proved incapable of following any conventional course of study or scheduling, even in graduate school. Learning had to be on my terms, to some extent, which I could only know by wrestling with the terms presented to me. That privilege was not available to everyone, but as a white child of the sixties, youngest in the family, of middle-class open-minded parents, I gradually understood (if only subconsciously) that the very form and pace and nature of my education was largely up to me, both in and out of school. Those institutions were there to serve me, as well as other students, and not for us to serve them. School loyalty never occurred to me. What was the point? I wasn't a flag-waver either. Such sentiments seemed meaningless in the greater light and aspirations of human fellowship.

What was that human fellowship, and how did it get mixed up with school? No one ever proffered the phrase to me, I don't think, in the halls of learning. I picked it up out of the dust somewhere, and as I turned it over, its relevance became clear as day amid the ambitions and rivalries that made up the trajectory of every student. Again, this was more instinct and intuition than an act of reasoning, yet my incessant curiosity about the where and how and what of human fellowship impelled me to step outside each circle, each school, each system that would have me. In the midst of my comforts, I still sought out the unfamiliar, the barely glimpsed, not knowing where my place really was—only where I was told it might be.

My academic career, as it unfolded, resembled a series of splinters at every turn, mostly of my own making, with me navigating the breaches anew. Who knows if I could have played it straight had I wanted to? Going to the Hebrew day school several miles from home, instead of the public school a few blocks away where my local friends went, initiated a quiet tension that led to the first break when, in the middle of third grade (a month or so after JFK's assassination), I was allowed to switch to Deal Elementary School for the rest of the year. Twice the size, it had two classrooms for every grade and a routine that was refreshingly secular. Still, I did not feel like I entirely fit in and besides I missed my Hillel School friends, so I returned there for fourth grade. But the divide would not be so conveniently ignored, now that I'd had a taste of freedom from religion, and by sixth grade my resistance got the better of me in the form of wisecracks and commentary launched at my Hebrew teachers. Getting thrown out of class seemed almost a badge of honor, and after a few visits to the principal's office I earned my second transfer, in the middle of that year, back to the local public school where I graduated two years later. Eighth grade provided a momentary lapse into conformity, for I nonetheless had my bar-mitzvah at the orthodox synagogue in Asbury Park where my family belonged and six months after was the only one of my school graduation ceremonies that I ever attended—though I retain no recollection of the event.

Like my brother and sister before me, I followed the normal pattern for our district and went to Asbury Park High School. From my white little town, that was a bit like joining the real world and I was all for it. Given the tenor of the times, that year also saw the school's first two student strikes: one led by Black students, demanding Black history and other relevant courses; and then, by those of us who were protesting the Kent State killings (for extra measure, we demanded the cancelation of final exams, which was granted). Meanwhile, I was beginning to learn the nuances of the color line in the north, in that my first girlfriend was Black; when we sat together in the lunchroom, few kids joined us. But my experience of a typical American high school was soon cut short when my father announced we were moving across the country to Berkeley in the summer, where both my parents had studied at the university and my brother was currently enrolled. From my perspective, it was as if I had transferred at age fourteen to a small liberal arts college: Berkeley High School was about five times the size of where I had been going, and the range of its offerings seemed unimaginable. Naturally, I found plenty of opportunities to veer away from a standard academic path, but with the multicultural experimental school I was engaged in much of that time and the courses in other programs with overlapping schedules at the high school, I was able to accumulate so many credits that I managed to graduate a year early. Days after the end of exams, at the height of my anti-intellectual intellectual rebellion, I set off with my banjo and backpack to follow the open road.

Nine months later, despite my initial reluctance, it was the banjo that led me to enter college at Berkeley, with a course on American folk song, as well as a survey of Black American literature. I started at an odd time in the calendar, spring quarter, but two years after that I was ready for a break and skipped the spring quarter to go travel in Mexico again, so that I ended up graduating at what would have been the normal time for my age. And though I took more courses in the English department than any other, I was not keen on the program required by their major, so I chose the option to devise my own. No surprise that it took me fourteen more years before deciding on graduate school, something I was quite certain I would never do, but by then I knew what I wanted to study for my doctorate, impractical as ever.

THE HOUR HAS LONG BEEN LATE

How incredible it all seems now, the story of the New World, of America. Ever more ships from Europe, full of palefaces; they arrive in a land that is obviously inhabited by other people and instead of approaching with humility to ask if they can live there too, they strike the ground and declare this land is theirs. Didn't anyone understand that is not a good way to start a country? Just show up and take over, you'll be fine. God is with you (no doubt a lunatic in a robe speaking).

But who has ever heard of such a thing, the invader comes and shows humility? What's that going to get him? On the other hand, isn't the fresh arrival supposed to be humble, trying to make sense of all the newness and maybe to fit in with what is already there?

In the pretense of a virgin land, the European knew he was terribly far from home. Never mind his weapons and his comrades, his prayers and his gods, never mind his king: Was he not scared? What did he give up in order to perpetuate that notion of home, though it surely lay elsewhere? Or if he would abandon his home, what did he gain in the process? The Europeans who became Americans wanted nothing more than to distance themselves from their ancestral origins; that was and was not who they were. Here, they could become someone else. In America, we discover, it is difficult to say who anyone really is: a list of descriptions, confused lineages, a character in a bitter comedy. They thought it was a land of boundless opportunities, not endless forgetting. The myth of a new start hangs over us either way, as if in answer to the spinning of the fates.

That new start, forced upon us or from plain dissatisfaction, may take a lifetime to achieve, even many generations. The conquerors end up vanquished by their own foolishness, their blindness and abuses: old story, shed no tears. The seeds that sprout and unfold within us do so in alternations of darkness and light, in mutable weather beyond our control that buffets us and caresses our skin and bathes us in the vivifying air of uncertainty. We are as trees moving through our forest, or as forests moving through our fog—except trees don't move, except they do, subsonically, immaterially, without letup, through birdflight and whiskers of wind and the echoes they absorb or paddle about amid the collective treemind. The new man and new woman dreamed of for the past few hundred years, in the old world and the new, have been moving among us, stirring within us all this time. Settlers, usurpers, profiteers who followed the bloody soldiers abroad, they soon understood the price of their wager. Their languages, after so much glory on the battlefields, could not conceive what they most needed. Dimly, deep behind the lid of consciousness, a faint noise taps about to say your gods cannot help you anymore, if they ever did: the changes you have wrought upon the material world have changed you irredeemably. Clear to see, yet somehow none the wiser. There is no going back now, only forward through your ruin.

CAT WALKING

He moves toward me at an angle as I advance, until causing me to stop and looks up at me. I see him and continue on my way except he remains planted, my path veering one, two steps to the side and veering still, his body posed sheer obstacle before me like a small bench to trip over. I halt enough to stretch one leg out, tacking past him as though against the wind; he doubles back to track obliquely further along and it is then I understand we are playing a match, although I may prove to be no challenge. Where was it I thought I was going, if that counts for any kind of direction. To think I might find myself outside the steps my own feet were taking, staring at the path that stretches forth untried. He blocks my way quietly waiting, so I veer off again, guided by the conviction that I had someplace to go. I could be mistaken, with each pivot he is making that clear, now I have an accent in my step that I don't recognize. Did he, on his four legs, do this to me? Still, I imagined that I, my legs were taking me across, over there, simple. But not simple: is that what those eyes blinking up at me are saying? Two steps here and one there, then one and one, or one and two, you don't know, until you get somewhere. He does not want me to take for granted the distance between two points. So, when he stands before me, smack in what I thought was the way, it may be he sees me as someone else. And no doubt I am. One who wasn't there a moment ago, but here, and here, buried in his certainties; who didn't realize what it all entailed walking over, until the cat showed up and made it clear.

Names from Elsewhere

A story I've told many times: when I was a kid at the Jersey shore in the sixties I didn't know of anyone else named Jason; except for one, a tall man possibly older than my father, who owned a deli in Asbury Park. I told my parents that I wished I had a more normal name, like Bob (a friend down the street) or Jeff (my brother, who was older and cool). Now, of course, we're everywhere, all ages and cultures. If a bunch of us were sitting in a room together, would we be musing about the strangeness of our name? As if it always gave us a way out somehow, a passage to some mysterious realm.

More often, as we know, names tend to reinforce the child's belonging to a community or family; and changing names, as for many immigrants, can be a way of fitting in. At a certain moment, our dentists molted before our eyes like that. First, Boris turned into Barry, and as he built up another office his wife Marina took over where we went; she was also a dentist and we were soon calling her Maureen. In Brooklyn they did this. We would have preferred to continue with their original names, but the choice wasn't ours. My father used to tell of a man he once knew who had changed one Eastern European Jewish-sounding last name for what seemed to be another. Was the guy crazy or just a fool?

I like to see names from multiple origins, as if to reflect the migrations real and imagined (I'm reminded that my daughter's name draws on three languages). And names that challenge me to pronounce them, to sound out the syllables at least in my head. Even the simplest names may stir us to imagine—a face, a life—almost instantly, as we move on. But to be a stranger to our own name in childhood, although bewildering perhaps, is to gain an early intuition for the wider world where everyone else is. Who is that traveler on the horizon? Probably he has my name too.

Pulling Up Stakes

For the first five years that I lived in Paris, through my late twenties, I preferred not to let on that I was American. I did not deny the fact or try to hide it, but I also did not advertise it in most of my habits. When a French woman once described me as Parisian, rather than a specific nationality, I was more than a little pleased. The many times Ali would say I'm not a typical American, I took that as confirmation. My early years there, I'd quietly walk past Americans lost on the street as they gazed about yapping loudly to each other. I felt almost as foreign among my compatriots as I did in not being French.

Even so, I did sometimes partake of a few American institutions in Paris—the American Center, for cultural events; the American Church, for its bulletin board with rental listings; and inevitably the *International Herald Tribune*, which I read mostly at kiosks and in the local library, and where I also worked now and then as a freelance cultural journalist. There was no sense of allegiance on my part in any of these interactions, simply that I knew they were available, among many other resources. Still, I felt on my guard when I walked through their doors, as if I didn't really belong in those places.

And yet, I was not against using that American identity as a cheap excuse occasionally. Foremost was a trivial detail that returns to me every year when the summer heat impels me to dress in shorts. I had always done that, in New Jersey and California the same. But in Paris come summertime, I began to realize that most European men— and from everywhere else—will always wear long pants, at least in the city. I felt too hot to put up with pants if I didn't have to, and since I wasn't working an office job I saw no need. Did it bother me that I might be perceived, on the street in summer, as almost surely American for that one detail alone? To hell with that, who cares, I was going to wear shorts.

When I first went off to Europe, I was excited by the places I was going to explore. It all felt like a new world, and even my uncertainties about its different habits and realities were stimulating. What took me longer to appreciate was how my native culture was implicitly kept at arm's length. More than arm's length, since that was pre-internet days. So, I was always a little ambivalent about meeting other Americans, both curiosity and suspicion stirred by their presence. In Paris, steering clear of Americans was a skill in itself, and most fully developed *by* Americans. As if some of us had concluded: not more than one or two at a time, please. That sentiment was not a program so much as a reflex of self-preservation.

Were we overreacting in avoiding our own kind? But were they our own kind, just on the basis of a passport? I admit it was nice sometimes to meet Americans abroad, though mostly it was disappointing. Americans tended to bring their America with them when they traveled, that's what I found, which made them often seem out of place. I liked to think I had not quite done so. Why go, why set off, if you're not going to leave where you came from? To frequent mostly Americans while in foreign lands seemed utterly pointless, without interest. What could I hope to learn in such an environment?

To live abroad, I realized, is to open yourself up to surprises—not just in the wealth of what you happen upon, but in your own thoughts and reactions and feelings. Surely this is far more the case if you go unattached, rather than being sent in the cocoon of the company you work for (because then you're just doing business) or even with a partner or family. We are speaking here of choice, clearly, and not of the forced exile or refugee. To the extent that I had a plan, it was to spend a year, half in Cadaqués and half in Paris, and who knows after that. The more I stayed in Paris, as the weeks turned to months, the more I wanted to stay. Before long, I thought I might well live there for the rest of my life. That year turned into a decade, at any rate, but eventually I wondered if maybe it was time to go, back to my native land. Nothing was really holding me there. Perhaps I was ready to learn from my compatriots again, for better and worse.

Something Other

Everywhere we turn, without a clue, we find objects abandoned, clothes never worn by their owners. Things orphaned, estranged, yet seeming just as they were, albeit misplaced. Or else, cheated of the life they were supposed to have. We would not know to recognize their past, nor where they belonged; we could not help them if we tried. However, sometimes a coat or a shirt, even though it was not meant for us, turns out to be our size and we walk away equipped for the seasons ahead. But that is just a lucky happenstance, nothing to rely on.

Our machines, like our loved ones, cannot help leaving survivors. After my printer broke down, I found on the shelf a set of new ink cartridges, forever unused. They had almost the value of what I paid for the printer. Was I a fool for stocking up? We are always left holding the bag, in the end. That's how the economy works. But to look at those ink cartridges, they were worse than useless. Their mere presence reproached me for the waste, and I could do nothing. Not so the good set of tires I bought months before my car's transmission fell apart; I will never see them again. I sold the carcass to my mechanic, and he passed it on to his manager who found a pricey used transmission and gave it to his wife for a city car. All to say, the tires will get used, if not by me. Ghostly objects, going places they would not have known in their old life.

For a while after my father died, a few years ago, my mother would offer items from his closet when I visited, whatever fit. His braided leather belt I wear every day, and often in winter I wrap myself in his black and white tweed overcoat, more than sixty years old. I have photos of him in that coat when he was still a young doctor. Three button-down summer shirts, I liked their colors, now hang in my closet optimistically. On the other hand, he stocked up too and so his new swimsuit, too large for me, finds no takers, unswum. And what of the socks, the sweaters still with their tags, dressing no one? Why not return them to the shelves of the store? They have no place in this world.

Nor does death need be the catalyst, fickle as we are, to transform an object into something other than it was intended to be. How many items do we acquire, we bring them home and promptly lose interest? Things left in corners until years later we get rid of them; easier to let them linger quietly, undemanding, their hopes of rediscovery a dim and fading glow. In their near non-existence, drained of purpose, they dwell in the shadows after our attentions have moved on. Such is the destiny of gifts we receive through the years, piling up like spent shells when the giving is done. Books, records, clothing, kitchen gadgets, jewelry, toys, they populate the house without anyone quite noticing. If they left on their own, to find a more appreciative home, we would be slow to realize.

We take things for granted, inevitably. How else to get through the day if everything were always fresh before our mind? We would be constantly overwhelmed. So, we must forget them a little, once we know them, or even before that. Sometimes, things fall out of range, our head makes room for other matters. When that's a foot we stop thinking about, nonetheless we continue to walk just fine. But when we trip, and look down at our foot as if it had betrayed us, we may have trouble remembering how to walk again.

TRANSIENT LIGHT

We were foreigners to each other and foreigners to the place, and we all loved being there as if it were the key to deep and luminous mysteries. Day in, day out by the sea, mystics and poets dreaming, painters drunk with every thing they saw. That jewel of a village, which one had to go over a mountain to get to, cast such an enchantment on visitors that their only wish was to stay. Timeless refuge, awash in Mediterranean light, we touched multiple histories there and yet it seemed a place to start anew. Or at least to step outside of where we had been.

I came to spend the autumn and winter in that village. It was a sort of experiment: I was twenty-three and had never lived abroad, only visited as a tourist the year before. I brought my trusted, lightweight Olivetti Lettera 32, and soon was writing a novel about a man who doesn't sleep, set in a similar landscape by the sea. An older American couple I knew, retired from the Foreign Service, introduced me to other people and so it went as I met residents from all over western Europe, a smattering of Americans, and an Argentine couple who became my closest friends. My artistic retreat could have easily slipped into a social scene, but mostly I was studious and avoided drama. Though I found my way to a few parties around the holidays, it was enough to remind me that the foreign population in the off season had a fairly limited circuit. At any rate, I was glad to spend some time away, and to meet people I would not otherwise encounter. I had no idea where all that might lead or how to appreciate it, just that I was starting to understand the importance of learning to be a stranger.

For Europeans maybe such lessons were no big deal—a jaunt down the road, a commerce of tongues, all in the normal course of things where countries are smaller and closer together. Even the Spanish speakers were outsiders, there in Catalan lands. For all our various desires to depart from our native territories, I knew precious little of what anyone left behind. Origin stories felt hardly pertinent to our discussions, except as an occasional reflection on current matters. If one person or another had made an actual break and fled from their past, I was not aware. Besides, most of the foreigners were older than me, at least in their thirties and well beyond, with children and not. The few people I knew my own age, also Americans, were like me on an extended stay before whatever came next. In a sense, we were neither here nor there, not much invested in the life of the place, unlike the permanent guests with their small businesses or retirement homes.

That village, then, was more a waystation for me, and (though I could not know it at the time) the site of many subsequent returns. Always catching the same bus over the mountain, I did not ever fail to marvel at the first sight, after yet another switchback in the descending road, of the gleaming facets of whitewashed houses before the wide embrace of the sea. The international community that came and went there—some to make their long last stand or to withdraw into an exquisite distance—found it to be one of those rare places where we might hope to shed, if only in the transient light, the cold defining contours of our origins. While the spell endured, all seemed right with the world, almost right.

POTOCKI

From the start of his "Mémoire sur l'ambassade en Chine" (1806), about a failed Russian delegation he was part of that never got past Mongolia, Jan Potocki makes it clear that Western arrogance was to blame most of all. Or at least in the persons of the ambassador and his first secretary. "Far from wanting to know the character of the Chinese," he writes, "they only seemed to care about showing them the sparkly side of European customs and surprising them with the seductions of our luxury." To that end, the ambassador puffs up the trappings of his own high importance and sets off belatedly from Irkutsk with a retinue of two hundred and forty people, which he considered "necessary for a man of his quality and rank." They get as far as the Mongolian border when he receives a letter from the king, on behalf of the emperor, who wants him to leave some of his large group behind. He is also asked for the list of presents he is bringing for the emperor, normal protocol. Potocki explains: "China being the most ancient empire in the world, the emperors consider themselves older brothers to all the kings on earth and demand of them not submission, but a certain deference." As the writer repeatedly shows, the ambassador and his advisors didn't much bother to do their homework.

Potocki, a Polish aristocrat with Ukrainian roots, who wrote in French and had produced extensive accounts of his travels through North Africa, the Mediterranean region, and the Caucasus, held a curious position in the delegation: ostensibly an advisor, he ended up more an observer. In 1805, he joined the Asian division of the Russian foreign affairs office, and soon was named head of the scientific section at the new Russian embassy in China, or so went the plan. He was forty-four years old. In the months prior to his departure that summer, he published several historical works and also the first small editions of early chapters from his singular delirium of a novel, *Manuscrit trouvé à Saragosse*, which would occupy him until the end of his life ten years later. His report on the troubled mission to China, twenty-six book pages long, was intended for government people back in Saint Petersburg, that they should know why it failed. He recounts the autumn months stuck at the border while the ambassador sends letters back and forth negotiating the size of his embassy. When at last a much-reduced retinue of seventy people is allowed to enter Mongolia, they are not sufficiently prepared for the severe winter. In the capital, Ulaanbaatar, they are delayed further as the ambassador continues to make a bad impression on the king by refusing to show him the same deference due the emperor, who eventually grows wary and declines their request to come to Beijing.

Ten months in all he was gone, so Potocki must have been more than disappointed to miss out on his chance to visit China. With the ambassador and the first secretary, their uninformed assumptions predictably undermining them, every move was the wrong move. And each time, we might well ask: if Potocki has an understanding of Chinese customs, why doesn't the ambassador? But further I wonder about the writer himself and the very long voyage he undertook in service to the government (and to his own insatiable curiosity, probably foremost). How long did he think he was going away to China, had the voyage gone as intended? Were his wife and small children going to join him there later? They could hardly be expected to make the journey themselves. And what of his marvelous novel that he was very much in the middle of at the time, did he bring all that with him? (In fact, he did: he wrote a new section of the novel by keeping to his room on the way there.)

The "Mémoire," we learn, is about an embassy that didn't exist; that attempted, in its clumsy way, to exist again after eighty years, but it wasn't going to happen under current leadership. The writer, providing his assessment to government policymakers as part of his role in the delegation, had become a different sort of traveler than he was in his many earlier voyages; more restricted by circumstances, the national entity he was working for. What did exist, as he conveys, was the bitter cold so extreme the mercury froze in the thermometers while they waited in Mongolia in their yurts trying to keep the fires stoked at all hours; and the soot infiltrating everywhere; and the monotony of the daily meal. How had they gotten to such a standstill! As the king tells the first secretary in the end, "I'll never understand you: we send you to Beijing and you seem to do everything possible to not go there."

If it weren't for these buffoons! Potocki must have been muttering some version of that phrase all the way back home. And yet, a cultured man, he would have nonetheless turned the experience to cultural profit. Always he had his books and research with him, even his drawing materials. But he also must have spoken at length with the keepers of the fire in the yurt, and with the king himself, and members of his court, and border officials, the interpreters too of course, and even with the cooks. How could he not ask and talk of all they had to say to him? Maybe none of it was written down, didn't have to be. He took it with him anyway.

The Going, Gone

Whatever approaches we may take to learning a language, imitation is the mode of transport coming and going. We imitate native speakers in order to shape our pronunciation more properly, and we seek to render a rhythm or a phrase as we hear it, the better to feel we are *in* the language. Like following a series of steps, imitation takes us a certain distance as we assimilate the language and discover how to use it. By taking such measures, we trust the native speakers as authoritative, more so for our purposes than the dictates of some abstract academy. All the way along, of course, there are gaps in our understanding, our knowledge and experience of the language, but gradually the gaps get smaller with practice until we can step over them almost without thinking.

In the early stages, though, we often have to fake it a little, as if we understand more than we really do. And yet we might, for on some barely conscious level a reflex of deductive reasoning helps to haul us along; comprehension, after all, has to do with more than just words. At any rate, we do not want to stop the flow, in our effort to tune into the language as it unfolds in the moment, even as we're stretching after the runaway train of the conversation.

But we like to talk, and to travel, and to meet new people. Why else would we learn another language? We're having a good time, someone tells a joke, we laugh, and then someone else follows on that, we laugh again. That's when the person beside us, having missed it, asks us to explain. It is not that we were pretending to catch the joke—although now that we are on the spot, who knows what went down in that instant—but maybe we misunderstood and were laughing at the wrong thing, or since everyone else saw the humor, it could have been the speaker's delivery that convinced us. Was it rather the condition of others' laughter that provided the cue for us to laugh too? Embarrassed that we cannot quite explain what was so funny, notwithstanding that we got all the words except possibly one, we play for time. Recounting any joke is perilous enough, let alone one apprehended on the fly and in a tongue where we are still a guest.

By trying to dissimulate, lest it seem we were found out in some deceit that happens to be untrue, we lose the thread in that quick turn of language as it unravels from our thoughts. The person beside us did not mean to test us like that and would sooner let the question drop than to see that breach opening before us. Except now we're called to account, we must attempt a response, for our own sake. Have we indeed mastered the adopted tongue? Did we manage to invent some loopy trick of meaning through seepage from that idiom? We understood the joke, we did, and the speaker's understated gesture that framed it. Spontaneous, a passing spark, it left hardly a trace among those taking part but for a small fold, a pocket of harmless shared complicity in which we were able to hold on as well, long as we did not look down, to notice our feet weren't touching the ground anymore.

Backward Glances

The nostalgia industry never got its claws much into me. I do not wish I lived in another time or place, or that I could return to an earlier moment in my own past; what would be the point? If happiness lay in the road not taken, the home abandoned, the love that was not forever, then we are all lost. To remember, to reminisce, is to stoke the possibility of unseen dangers if we forget where we are now and how we got here. Only the present seems a mess; the past appears all settled, even inevitable, whether or not we see it in its just proportions. But the temptation to revisit our past tugs at every turn.

Like many another who's wandered far enough into the weeds of middle age, I began to grow curious about people I was friends with in childhood and high school. Who had they become, and what was their situation now? Where did they settle, and—though I would not ask directly— had they gone over to the dark side of the idiot hordes? So, I contacted several and a few found me as well. What are we looking for, do we know? Reaching out across time and space like that, without aiming to return to the past exactly, we are venturing to retrieve something and bring it into the light of the present to examine once more—

an affection, a rapport that somehow radiated all the way to this moment. How has its meaning changed? That we and those certain others are still alive in this world would seem to demand a kind of recognition. By making contact again, our curiosity gets the best of us and we might well let it fly while we can. For me, in those various instances of renewed communication, the encounter often did not get past email and at that, after two or three exchanges back and forth, it tended to peter out. My own inclination, when possible, is to entertain the potential for an ongoing dialogue, at whatever irregular pace might establish itself, but most of my correspondents had no room, or time, or interest, to sustain any real engagement. That may have been just as well, let sleeping dogs lie if they're not going to roll over and talk. Is it that we're safer as strangers to each other? Why look back, after all, why seek after the paths we turned away from?

That temptation of the backward glance, with all its risks, finds its most common expression in the class reunion. For years I resisted. As if to steel myself against such exercises, I even accompanied my wife to a couple of her reunions. These proved mildly amusing, but only because I was a mere accessory. It was another two decades before I went to one of my own, at Deal Elementary School. Being a small local public school in a well-off town, the reunion covered not just one year's class but people who had attended over a span of two decades. The fact that I went to the school for just a few years, and that my family left the area a year after I graduated from eighth grade there, made me less rooted in the particularities of the place. What's more, I shared in none of the events that soon defined the area: the race riots that erupted in Asbury Park days after I got on the plane, and three years later the first album and subsequent career of the local rock star who carried a whole swathe of culture in his wake. At the reunion, in any case, such markers were hardly on the minds of people who remembered me, only that I left early, went off to California, while everyone else remained... in New Jersey. Though no one seemed to question why did I return, surely those divided loyalties conditioned my uncertain presence there.

What struck me, nonetheless, was the persistence of old patterns; or more like ancient patterns. It would be easy to imagine a similar small-mindedness in villagers five hundred years ago, that general lack of curiosity about the one who went away and what they found abroad, almost a lingering and unspoken resentment. I cannot say with any certainty that such sentiments were in force on some level, but I found no desire in anyone I spoke with to get beyond initial pleasantries, no opening sought to do more than touch on a few threadbare memories. Worse, old prejudices remained inexcusably intact. At one point, I was standing with a few guys I had known a bit as kids, and one asked another who a woman was that they'd noticed across the room. "I don't know," shrugged the Manhattan lawyer, "some Syrian." In the years after I left, more and more Sephardic Jews had moved into town, overtaking the Ashkenazi population. As the evening was winding down, I realized that one or two childhood friends had already taken off. Someone else explained that people were meeting up over at the Wonder Bar in Asbury Park where a few of those I knew were going to do a set playing their electric guitars. So, I left the reunion alone, with no one really to say goodbye to, feeling like more of a ghost than when I had arrived. Once I found a parking space near the bar, I hesitated to get out of my car. I remembered I didn't like rock clubs, where I'd have to shout over the noise to attempt any conversation, assuming we found something further to say to each other. Besides, none of them had bothered to invite me directly. Did it matter to anyone whether I showed up? I started the engine and drove away, to the house of friends I was staying with, a few towns further.

THE STRANGENESS OF BOOKSTORES

It should naturally be my home. And yet it's not. Familiar as the elements may be, I find little comfort there, no place I recognize as my own. Across the bright, burgeoning shelves, the sumptuous tables, all is mute before my eyes, uninviting. The smart designs and colorful titles, in their dignified party, seem to make no room for me. Look, it's him, they might whisper, maybe he'll go away. Don't you know you don't belong here among us? That's the problem, I'm the sort who never quite gets the message; who keeps coming back, wide-eyed, susceptible to the hope of chance encounters, waiting for a welcome. What could be more ridiculous than a book turned inside out, its pages exposed, spilling its secrets to whomever will listen? We step around such obstacles, resentful of the imposition. But I refuse to make a spectacle of myself. My anonymity gets the best of me; do I even cast a shadow?

The articulation of an identity, for a writer, is an especially slippery operation. There is no end to it, publishers and publicists notwithstanding. We are not our books, although. Most likely some resemblance does accrue (we've lived with them so intimately), even if the crowd pleaser on paper is not the same in person. Still, for anyone unknown to the writer—the public, potential readers—the books seem a hint of the person; the very existence of the writer takes on some external form, at least in thought, as if conjured by the audience. And yet how partial is that knowledge, a small part often enough, with which to project a figure.

But I don't have that luxury of an external form, or so I tend to feel. Though I have published some books, and appeared occasionally in public to read from my work or talk on one or another subject, I still have a hard time imagining there is anyone I don't know who has read something I've written. Compounded upon that is the fact that my more creative works remain unpublished, books that quite amused me as I dreamed and labored over them, that I thought could well amuse others. It would seem I really had no clue. The books that have managed to come out were thought to interest only a very limited, specialized audience, which was probably true, and so they were printed in editions of one or two thousand copies. A few I glimpsed in some bookstore at first, but that didn't last long. If I have any identity as a writer, it is to be found as much as anywhere in the works of imagination, however imperfect, unknown to all but one or two friends.

So, decades and decades of writing might almost

have passed in a dream. I have never had a sense of "my readers," but rather that I was sending messages in a bottle to mysterious recipients, out there somewhere. Who knew when or if those messages would land, or how far they would have to bob along until their discovery? Entering a bookstore, therefore, is neither an innocent nor an easy act for me. Naturally, I keep my cool, though the experience could soon turn out to be overwhelming. Those many, many shiny new volumes: how did all those writers get their books published, when I can seldom manage to do so? And if my own work isn't much found in stores, how do I persist in thinking it could or should be? What manner of delusion maintains its hold on me that I keep writing regardless? You would think a man would come to his senses after long enough.

Leaving aside the fate of my own productions, it is rather sobering to see the quantity of new titles that come out every season. My, people are busy; I better get busy too, or busier. Nor am I a reliable customer: with no room left on my shelves at home, and the piles of still-unread books inching ever higher, I cannot justify adding to the burden, or obligation, or the surfeit of temptations. Which does not stop me from acquiring some tome now and then, in the right conditions or the unexpected branching of my curiosity. But there is a further aspect to the incongruities of my wandering through a bookstore, since I am often less inclined toward current titles than following after one or another path back through the past or into some obscure precinct that is unlikely to justify its place on the shelves of present-day commerce. I am not trying to cultivate a taste for the arcane, or to pretend that what lies before me doesn't matter, but standing in the store may awaken my contrarian reflex: all those choices on display, sparkling with critics' praises, there within reach if I only decide; must they determine what I read next? Is that all there is, I sometimes wonder—not in disdain of what may be on offer, for I've hardly ventured to try them out. Instinctively, I question what got left out, what's missing from the fashions of the moment, and the benefit in so doing, thanks to that fountain of choices, is that it sends me back upon my own resources, reminds me what I have already, whether in the unread stacks at home or bubbling quietly in my head, awaiting the keys of happenstance and grudging distraction. And so, entering the bookstore was not for naught, though I had no known purpose for the occasion. Unaware, forces were fine-tuning their alignments, beneath the noise of my worried resistance.

The Lingual Sea

It took me a long time, past thirty, before I ever thought of living in New York. To me, growing up at the Jersey shore, the big city seemed much too daunting. Later, on the contrary, as a high school and college student in Berkeley, I was rather put off by that arrogant place that thinks it's the center of the universe. Only when I was living in Europe and had been coming back to visit every couple of years, did I begin to see New York on a human scale, because friends lived there. Even so, I wasn't tempted by the idea of such a move.

Distractions have a way of telling us what we need to know sometimes. So it was for me, riding the subway on those visits. How many times my eyes must have roamed over the ads in the subway cars, one day I realized what I was seeing and took comfort. I noticed many ads were in two languages, and for public service announcements even in three or four: English, Spanish, Chinese, Kreyol. Part of what I loved about the foreign city where I lived was the sense of so many languages weaving through the air together. Somehow I felt at home in that atmosphere. Those ads reminded me what anyone knows about New

York, except it gets drowned out beneath all the noise about power and glory.

But this is not about New York really. The refuge of languages has sustained me since I was a teenager when I came to understand that there were other worlds, other dialogues to inhabit alongside what was given as innately my own. When I write in Spanish or French—to friends, or exchanging information, or occasionally for publication— with my imperfect mastery of the idiom, somewhere I remember that I'm leaving behind the American, English-only realm, and that gives me encouragement. After four-plus decades swimming back and forth, I am still a bit surprised to find my thoughts dressed in a language that once was unknown to me. Did I stumble through a hidden door? Writing confirms my departure in such moments, as I engrave word upon word across the page in signs that will be understood by the appropriate parties, if not by most people where I came from.

As a general literary practice, I would not presume to write in other than my native tongue, unless conditions warranted it—if I lived permanently in a foreign land perhaps or it was a secret writing, like the French poetry of César Moro, the Peruvian writer. Thinking in another tongue turns out to be less a problem than bouncing around between one and the other, tracking two distinct rhythms and structures of articulation. So, to translate my own text from English into French, as I do occasionally, is like a wrong-way adventure filled with puzzlements the more I peer at the details. A tightrope walker glancing at his feet, my balance wavers. I have to be able to trust my ear, as it measures out approximations of a phrasal swing, but soon my English ends up looking funny to me; or, I get impatient with the original writer, me, and find myself taking liberties with the French. Who's to say no?

I am one of those people who prefer to live near water. But the proximity of a lingual sea, a flow of many tongues, came to feel long ago just as essential for my well-being. That perspective has not had much resonance in the Anglo-American world. What matters, for me, is the accessibility of an exit, a point of departure, the prospect that I may yet evade the box thrown up around me. Through language we can step outside a while, become almost strangers again, and thus postpone any physical leaving. It might be we never go, thinking of that great stretch of water rolling on, ready to take us.

STRAYS

I've just received a package in the mail, on this snowy afternoon, postmarked two weeks earlier in Ankara. The brown paper wrapping was torn open in every corner, but I knew what it was, so I was glad for the clear plastic envelope that the US Postal Service had sealed it in. I'd been half-expecting the package—or at least aware of its possible arrival, if it actually came to exist—for a long time, though it might be endlessly delayed in reaching me. And so, there they were: three thick copies of the Farsi translation of my first book, from 1991—a mere twenty-seven years later—interviews with writers in Paris in the 1980s. The new edition was published in Tehran, where the translator lived until recently.

Arash first sent me an email almost six years ago, out of the blue, to explain that he was halfway through translating the book and that he would probably want to ask me about some details. He mentioned in passing that most often the original authors and publishers in Western countries are never told of such editions, since for one thing there is no possibility of payment. For that he apologized in advance and also because the independent literary press that he thought would publish the translation was only likely to print at most 1,500 copies. I was delighted, of course, and replied that the original print run was not even that much. I had so many questions though held off, perhaps out of discretion; besides, our infrequent correspondence had enough to cover with the matters at hand.

But, for instance, how did he ever chance to find my book, and what got into his head that he would undertake such a thankless task? As my son put it, if he was able to read the book in English, why did he decide he had to translate it too? In the US at least, a translator's enthusiasm for a work rarely suffices for a publisher to commit to bringing it out. Beyond all that, who was going to buy my book in Iran? How were such readers likely to know about it, and where would they find it? Obviously, the questions were the same everywhere. Of the nine writers I interviewed, mostly European and Latin American, nearly all had serious literary reputations in the West, but what did that mean in Iran? Did it count extra?

Certainly, I understood that securing a publisher might prove difficult, just as it had been for me in the States. From the start, I told my friends—that book seemed the most unexpected, out of this world thing to happen to me, and even provoked a bit of awe that it could happen. All the more so, two months ago, when Arash sent me as an email attachment the cover of the book, which I could recognize only because over the bottom fifty-five percent of the page (mustard yellow background), in three rows of three circles each, like portholes, were photos of the writers I had interviewed. I'd seen most of those photos before, but none were from the batch I sent to him electronically. The next day, I forwarded the attachment to friends, and some even cheered me on as if I had done something subversive, citing the kind of lists it will get me on. In any case, that book suddenly became more real—wherever it existed in the world, if it existed yet, and however it was to be found—by the mere evidence of what seemed to be a cover. And because Arash told me so. But were there really more than a few people to read the book in Persian?

Now with a copy on my desk, I marvel at the strange object before me. It is and is not mine. With more heft than the original, many more pages; also, more austere, in that the only images at all are those nine author photos on the cover, each in their circle as if spotted through a telescope. My old friend Ali confirmed to me which two words above the photos were my name. Inside, beyond the ISBN information on the copyright page, I understood not a word. In the abstract, it seemed to me a rolling sea of writing, upon which I might happily get lost for days on end. Right to left I knew, yet no matter how long I plunged in through the pages with their endless mystery, I grew no closer to reading the language. And then on one page, bobbing among the waves, I stumbled across a few snippets in English from Brion Gysin's permutations of the divine tautology, I am that I am. In fact, Brion went to Iran back in the mid-1970s to see the nearly inaccessible fortress at Alamut where Hassan-i-Sabbah, the Old Man of the Mountain, held sway over his assassins nine hundred years before; so, I was pleased to realize that I had helped facilitate a sort of return trip for Brion, thirty-two years after his death. But that was all quite removed from the book at hand, was it not? In truth, I didn't know. I didn't know what was in my own book except open doors, for those who could see them, and the fulfillment of a desire. Like any writer translated into an unknown language, I could only go on faith that the genetic stamp of the original work had carried through—which means, naturally, that like one's children it also changes in unexpected ways, grows new connections in a different time and place, transports us where we least imagined.

But even without the self-effacing labors of a translator, that book has surprised me in its travels. Six months after its publication, I received a letter from Basra: Hussein, a professor emeritus of literature, had seen notice of it somewhere and was eager to read it. As I recall, he explained his difficulties obtaining a copy in Iraq, so I sent him one. I was sure he confirmed receipt, though digging now through my files which are no doubt incomplete I find a curiously more complicated story. Three typed letters between April 1992 and July 1993, and one more, handwritten from Libya much later. Think of what was happening in Iraq as well as Libya in those years, and here was a retired literature professor thinking about my book, of all things. In the first letter already, he makes reference to a previous request five months earlier which I clearly had not received, and in closing offers a sort of ages-old flourish with contemporary relevance: "I do hope that eventually in this world sanity and love will return, not just for our sake but for our children," and finally, "from the other side of the world, I wish you lasting peace and happiness." How could a peace and love kind of guy not send him a book? Apparently, that was no easy task; his next letter, eleven months later, thanks me for my own letter two weeks before, saying it's the first he ever received from me. He recognizes from what I said that I'd written to him previously and also that I must have looked into sending the book to Basra but found it impossible due to the trade embargo. So, he asks if I might send it instead to a friend of his in Ma'rib, Yemen, who would be back in Basra in three months. But four months after, he writes to say that he saw his friend who just returned and never received the book in Yemen. He makes his request once more and notes: "it might be warming for you to know that in this tortured, war-weary country, in a city that has suffered so terribly, scholarship flourishes and Literature remains a bright, guiding light." Though I cannot find any written evidence, I'm pretty sure I sent him the book once or twice in that period and that he received it; or maybe not. Nearly a decade passed before I heard from him again, in November 2002, writing from exile in Misurata, Libya. There he reminds me about his letters from Basra and Sana'a to "[communicate his] desire to receive a copy of your beautiful book," and "[begs] your favor" for a "used copy." He closes with more wishes for world peace and the sense that in writing to me he is "struck by how close— not how far—one continent is to another and one culture is to another." So, I sent him one more copy of the book. I wonder where did the stray copies go, tattered under rubble by now or else who knows lost on some bookshelf in a faraway land.

We continued our correspondence by email in the winter and spring of 2003, when I sent him a new book as well. Both books got there eventually. "I wrote to you from Basrah (!!) when I was single, and today my daughters … thank you for your kindness." The family had left home in September 1993, he explained, spent two years in Yemen, and then in Libya ever since. He was enthusiastic about the American invasion to get rid of Saddam, and anticipated being able to return soon. I don't know quite when they did, but he wrote to me once more from Basra in January 2015, when he read of a new book of translations I'd published. "I greet you from the patient land." He sent me photos of his two grown daughters, himself, and his wife, before one of the daughters went off to do graduate studies in Turkey, for a master's in geology.

WERE WE EVER THERE

If my daughter or son ever did what I had done at sixteen—hitchhike around the country for four months—I'd have been constantly sick with worry. Did I not consider my own parents back then? It is a different country now, meaner in a noxious way, and far fewer drivers will even pick up hitchhikers. Those that do, there might be good reason to question their motives. Besides, the hitchhikers themselves may be more questionable; likely more desperate, with nothing to lose. The old pact of strangers sharing a ride, for company and convenience, hardly seems possible anymore before the threat of gruesome probabilities. Gone are the days of good-natured wanderers sticking their thumb out by the side of the road; or if not gone entirely, eclipsed by ominous clouds.

When I ventured forth on that long ago voyage, I thought I was off to discover America—for myself. Ever perplexing land, ever kind and cruel. In my many encounters, somehow it escaped me that I was traveling a foreign land. We all spoke the same language more or less, maybe that's what I misunderstood. How did I end up in Weiser, Idaho, or Austin, Minnesota, or South Cushing,

Maine, each quite different from the places I had known? Were they, by some arcane calculus, more authentic places? There was no reason to think so except they were new to me. Months earlier, I had no idea they existed. I remembered the connections that led me to those towns, the roads and the rides and the people I befriended, but I was only passing through. I couldn't imagine belonging there really. That wasn't the point of my journey, anyway: I wanted to glimpse other people's lives, in places I wouldn't have visited save by chance or the hazards of planning.

How did I have the slightest inkling where to go, once I left home? I had just graduated early from high school, and before the week was out, with my backpack and banjo (in a guitar case stuffed with extra clothes), I was on my way to the annual fiddle contest in Weiser—pronounced Weezer, which gave it an extra glow. By the lights of Woody Guthrie and Jack Kerouac, I was looking to see the world. Like anyone who travels long distances, I plotted out a number of possible points across the land, by way of music interests, friendships, and past lives. Where would I sleep each night, beyond my down sleeping bag, was a blank to fill in only when I got there. Not sure where I heard of the famous old fiddle contest, could have been a gathering of the San Francisco Folk Music Club at Faith Petric's Victorian on Clayton Street in the Haight or else my folk music friend Patty Hall; in any case, Patty introduced me to a lady whose name I forget—in her fifties, salty sort, called her Toyota sedan Tillie—and she was driving up to Weiser, meeting up with her boyfriend, Virgil Evans, a California state fiddle champ. I helped with the driving, it took the entire day. Many of us at the festival slept in the park.

An informal jam session is likely where I met Wayne, a long-haired guitar player from Louisville, Kentucky, who had worked with some noted musicians back home. We hitchhiked together north out of Weiser and spent the night at the home of a couple he knew who had a converted schoolhouse in Sandpoint. From there we continued hitching on up into Canada the next day and parted ways when I turned east toward Banff and he went west. He had told me he was gay, unusual enough for a country music player from Kentucky in 1972, with that American Jesus look of the time, but when he wrote me six months later that he'd become a Jehovah's Witness, I didn't know what to say to him anymore, like he'd turned into a Martian. The next place I had sights on was Austin, several days away, where a girl I knew from Berkeley High School, Peggy Holmes, was going to be back staying with her family. I don't recall exactly her situation, had trouble with school and through some relative or whatever managed to enroll in high school in Berkeley. I got along swell with her mother and sister, had a brief flirtation with her friends Gina and Sandy, and we spent the Fourth of July with a couple who lived outside of town—he worked at the Hormel plant and they had a kid—after passing half the day at a swimming hole where some of us jumped in from a cliff high above (or was I mistaken on that last jump and ever since this life has been all just a—never mind). Fifteen years later in Paris, I befriended another native of Austin, a poet named Robert, and we traveled to Poland together.

Ten days further, in my American voyage, I got a ride from someone I knew. At the Mariposa Folk Festival in Toronto, on an island in Lake Ontario, I ran into Faith Petric and she introduced me to Jean Ritchie, famous in traditional music. They were driving east through New York state and offered to take me; I was going as far as Syracuse, and much of the way I did the driving (a sixteen-year-old kid was entrusted with driving a Folkways recording artist?). In Syracuse, I stayed a couple days at a house of university students where my sister's ex-boyfriend had lived, and then one of them gave me a ride east to Albany, where I caught up with the Clearwater, the Hudson River sloop, to begin a week of volunteer work on board. I left the boat in Beacon and hitched south to a summer camp near Budd Lake, in New Jersey, where Patty and her brother and sister were working (ten years ago, she gave me a recording from that time, of me playing the banjo there and singing). In that play of echoes across time which makes a familiar place unexpectedly new again, sixteen years later I met my future mother-in-law who lived a few miles from that camp. When my wife and I got married a couple years after on her mother's property, my father told me that his parents and other immigrant Jews from Jersey City and nearby towns used to rent summer bungalows around Budd Lake.

All travel, I suppose, lays down a kind of mapping for the future. For one thing, new elements are constantly introduced, however they come into the picture, and we don't know if they will rise in prominence for us or fall away completely. Those elements may be people, or towns, or landscapes, or occupations; they may even be words, a scent, an angle of eye or ear. One more folk festival I attended, Fox Hollow, in upstate New York, at the lovely Beers Family estate in Petersburg near the Vermont and Massachusetts borders. It was held a month after Mariposa, early-mid August, and there I saw Patty again who presented me to several seasoned performers I'd heard on record. Other people I met at the festival led, in turn, to the next three stops in my travels, going east along Route 9 through Vermont and beyond. Or I may have the itinerary confused, since I went other places too, including down to the Jersey shore once or twice to stay with my first girlfriend and her family, though I seem to recall from Fox Hollow getting a ride with musicians I knew from the San Francisco scene and the Boys of the Lough group in another car, all of us headed for Marlboro and Margaret MacArthur's house (*Folk Songs of Vermont*, 1962), where in some corner or other I was put up for the night. But I also visited a girl from the festival who went to college at Bennington, which is west of Marlboro, stayed a night on a couch in her student co-op; eastward, in New Hampshire north of Concord up some road, I caught up with others from the same group of festivalgoers. These people were a bit older and worked as counselors at some kind of alternative group home for nominally troubled teens hardly younger than me, funded who knows why by the state of Massachusetts. Everyone lived in a cluster of houses with barns and workshops, a place they called Rivendell. The people I had met turned out to be Christian Scientists, for some reason, though they seemed otherwise normal. One of them was also a skilled blacksmith. In my days there, I got along well with both the kids and the counselors, trying to help out where I could, my banjo close at hand.

Who in the world travels like that now? It's crazy, presumptuous, naïve. Perhaps I was already from a lost time. Whether my visit to Rivendell happened then or a month later, it was about that time of late August that I continued east to South Cushing, Maine, to stay with Sally Smith's family at their summer home. A month earlier on the Clearwater we had worked together. That week, I ate lobster twice, with fifteen at table the last time, once her older sister and brother came home from jobs at summer camp and brought friends. In between, I cooked omelets on the beach for some of us with clams we dug out of the sand. I thought I might stay the winter in Maine working on boats, had a letter of recommendation from the captain of the Clearwater. But I didn't do that, in the end. Come mid-October, I flew back to Berkeley from Boston as it was beginning to get cold, still not thinking of college.

La Habanera

The cascading ironies of a film production, its principal talents, its moment in time, and the surrounding circumstances, could not be more pronounced than in Detlef Sierck's musical melodrama *La Habanera* (1937). A German film with a Spanish title, it traded in the exotic only to serve as a hackneyed warning. The German-born director, who emigrated before the film's release at the end of the year, was soon to be known when he reached Hollywood as Douglas Sirk. Of Danish parents and married to a Jewish woman, he made the film for UFA, then under Nazi control, shooting partly at the company's studio in Potsdam-Babelsberg; it was not his own project. The story had ostensibly nothing to do with Germans but rather a dark-haired Swedish woman who happily goes astray in Puerto Rico. Never mind that the *habanera* music she finds so enticing suggests a different island in the same sea and of the same language, a distinction of no importance since everyone's speaking and singing in German. What matters, in the end, at least for the National Socialists, is that the remorseful Astrée, ten years wiser, returns to her homeland with her very blond son. Conveniently, she is released from her domineering though once gallant husband, Don Pedro, when he is struck down by the dreaded "Puerto Rico fever." Driving the point home, one of her own countrymen rescues her, Dr. Sven Nagel, an old beau who has traveled to the pestilential paradise to find a cure. Which he does, in no time flat; if it weren't that the jealous Don Pedro has it destroyed before they get any further.

For a country bent on a sick sense of nationhood at the time, boasting a fictive purity that would be laughable were it not so deadly, *La Habanera* was a popular entertainment with a purpose; little wonder that the writer became a member of the party. And yet, the whole enterprise was riddled with cultural borrowings and sleights of hand, to such an extent that the propaganda machine should have collapsed under the weight of its own contradictions. If the island didn't matter, the sea didn't either, given that the exterior scenes were shot more easily in Tenerife, the Canary Islands, off the coast of North Africa. Which explains how the décor, the dress (except for the shepherd boy in a loincloth), the movements seem decidedly Spanish rather than Caribbean. Authenticity may have been irrelevant in the crafting of a message, but even the lead actors couldn't manage to be good Germans. Ferdinand Marian (born Haschkowetz) was Austrian—close enough, considering—and the same physical aspect that enabled him to fit the part of Don Pedro, the generic Latin lover, gained him the title role a few years later in the viciously anti-Semitic film *Jud Süss* (Suss the Jew). In effect, he never lived it down, dying a year after the war either from drunk driving or suicide on the way to picking up his denazification papers. Coerced by Goebbels to take the part, his personal life suggested quite a different character: his first wife was Jewish, with whom he had a daughter, and his second wife had also been married to a Jew, whom they hid in their home.

Swedish singer and actress Zarah Leander, by contrast, lasted until the early 1980s, ever a controversial figure. Her greatest success was in Germany in the '30s and '40s, and in 1936 she signed on as a contract player with UFA where she made ten films; even so, two years later she recorded the Yiddish chestnut "Bei Mir Bistu Shein." Color her confused. Astrée would seem a role tailor-made for her, the German-speaking Swede, as both the actress and her fictional counterpart carefully steered clear of local politics. Her stardom may have protected her for a while, but when her Berlin home was bombed in an air raid in 1943, she chose to return to Sweden. For the rest of her life, she insisted she had had no sympathy for the Nazis and was simply an entertainer. That may well have been: a career untouched by an agenda, untroubled by a moral center. But long after she was gone, claims arose that she had actually been a Soviet agent and was also a member of the Swedish Communist Party.

In its story, the film reinforced a principle that one should find strength and salvation in one's own kind. But real life was too messy for such delusions. Sirk knew that as well as anyone. His first wife, a decade earlier, subsequently joined the Nazi party and was able to bar him from seeing their son because Sirk's second wife was Jewish; the son, meanwhile, became a leading child actor in Nazi-era cinema, but eventually became a soldier and died at the Eastern Front, still a teenager. Likewise, the little blond boy who played Astrée and Don Pedro's son Juan, in his only film role, was drafted before the end of the war and killed at seventeen fighting for the fatherland.

WELCOME

My first morning in New Orleans started out simply enough. At the corner market, I bought a bite of breakfast and a pint of orange juice and went to sit on a bench in the leafy square across the way. It was the middle of May and already warm at that hour. Soon, a Japanese woman sat nearby, took a few snapshots, gestured to ask if I minded, and I responded I did not. We attempted a minimal conversation, not speaking each other's language, and before departing she gave me a pretty Japanese coin with a hole in the middle, which I kept long after.

I had hitched in from Houston the day before and found my way to The Head Inn, a youth hostel in the French Quarter. I was nineteen and had taken the spring term off college to travel. After depositing my backpack at the hostel, I wandered the streets of the district, not interested in paying to go hear tourist jazz, content to see what I could. The achievement that evening was to chance upon a well-known spot for red beans and rice, where I was doubly impressed to find they had John Coltrane on the jukebox.

But no, I have it backwards: my encounter with the Japanese lady was the second morning, the quiet epilogue to this tale as I sought a moment's refuge in the leafy square, bleary-eyed from lack of sleep. The corner store was separate, the site where it began. I emerged with my orange juice alongside a blond kid I'd just met there, who turned out to be from Jenner, my neck of the woods approximately, up the California coast in Sonoma County. We hadn't exchanged more than a few words when a small pickup truck pulled to the curb and the driver stepped out: "You guys looking for work? We're setting up a carnival across town." A muscly fellow in a leather vest, he wasn't going to linger. Luke didn't hesitate, and I barely did either, we hopped in the back of the truck and off we went. Where we were going, we had no idea, nor who the mystery woman was up front beside him. A minute later, we were sailing down the highway, the warm air blowing through us, and a few miles further we were turning through streets I would not have guessed were the same city.

We drove onto a lot amid half-risen carcasses that would, through the afternoon, turn into rides like the Tilt a Whirl. The woman got out of the pickup dressed in leopard-spot pants with a matching handbag and smoking a black cigarette holder. The man at the wheel, taller and younger, introduced her as Miz Becky and himself as Tiger. She was the owner of the operation and past forty; I thought I noticed a small Star of David around her neck. He brought me over to a very tall longbeard they called Little John, a wry lumbering sort who provided tools and a belt and showed me a series of bolts I had to fasten onto a network of metallic arms and struts. Were these erector sets assembled by the likes of me—though I did have some mechanical skills—actually safe? I didn't ask. We worked steadily on our tasks, and as the carnival took shape clusters of kids would gather here and there to look on, make comments, pose idle questions. The housing projects across the street must have been home to a lot of families. Surely it would have made more sense to take on a few local people than to go hire Luke and me and whoever else as extra hands.

Toward the middle of the lot a small trailer was parked which served as the office: that was where Miz Becky reigned and sold tickets. We finished setting everything up by late afternoon and around six they were open for business. The whole enterprise was new territory for me. I hadn't attended so much as a state fair, and here I was suddenly a mechanic, ticket collector, operator of rides.

Plenty of summers I had enjoyed the amusements on the boardwalk at Asbury Park, and visiting my grandparents each year in Santa Cruz the same, but I had never seen the itinerant version or passed through to the other side among the people who made it happen. The kids and the families of the neighborhood had waited long enough, they were eager to have fun, to check out what this motley bunch had in store for them, while I moved about helping wherever I was needed, in any position that Little John, or Tiger, or Miz Becky thought to place me.

Once the carnival was under way, I hardly had time to focus on the constant movement and the countless new faces, let alone their relationships to each other or who they might be. What I did notice early on there was that every last visitor through the day as we worked was a person of color, while all of us setting up these contraptions were not. I didn't know if that was a normal situation for where I was, in 1975, but I said nothing and kept my ears open. It wasn't so much the language I picked up as the growing annoyance among some of the crew at the kids who hung around watching us. There must be better things to do for employment, I thought. Even so, the first few hours Miz Becky and Tiger had the carnival cranking along like a well-oiled machine, though I wasn't too clear how late it was expected to go that night. There was a sort of pleasant delirium in being part of that machine, for a short while, and I didn't think much about what was next except that my backpack was still at The Head Inn.

It wasn't yet ten when I became aware of shouting amid the great din, and slowly every element of the cacophony—the speaker system, the big engines, the swinging of large metal limbs—ground to a halt. The shouting was still going on, clearly that was Miz Becky's voice screaming and Tiger making chase, but the kid already got away with Miz Becky's purse which had been sitting on a shelf by the door. He ran off toward the projects, someone said, and I was close enough to see a group of kids by the ticket window gazing on with surprise. Luke the Californian took a step forward and challenged them: "Who did this? You know who did this!"

What were they going to do, Tiger and Miz Becky? Was it true most of the proceeds were in her purse? How was it possible to regain any semblance of that mad equilibrium? From one moment to the next, all of us in that lot had become strangers again, our movements rendered abstract, without clear purpose. We waited for some kind of signal, our eyes trained on the two principals of the operation. They didn't confer much, Miz Becky adamantly shaking her head. "That's it, it's over!" Tiger shouted, waving his arms. "We're taking it all down! Not going to stick around here another day, we're done!"

Miz Becky climbed back into the trailer. At the window, she was inconsolable. "You people didn't want it! What am I supposed to do?"

They had offered me fifty dollars for the day. Clearly I wasn't going to see that now. Tiger came up to me as if to explain, but I tossed my hands up saying I understood, I was going to help them take it down. All through the night I labored with those bolts and wrenches, and fighting the mosquitoes which seemed more ravenous under the glare of the floodlights than they had been at dusk. I don't know how I paced myself with each hour and only when dawn rolled over us did I feel how tremendously weary I was.

We had taken apart everything there was to disassemble, and aware I wouldn't last much longer it was all I could do to take my leave of people and get myself up onto the highway to hitchhike back in to the French Quarter.

Tiger offered a five-dollar bill in token compensation; I waved it away.

By the side of the road, I could barely stand up and after a while when no one stopped I sat down in the dirt, still sticking my thumb out. One last time I rallied, knowing I was almost there, and stood up again until I got a ride. I struggled not to fall asleep in the car.

SPANISH DAYS

Alphie from Wordland. Or rather, Alphonse; almost Alfonso, the word wise. Van Worden the surname, Dutch: to become, to get to be, to grow, to turn. Alfie from Becoming. Anagram: wonder. But of course—so is noble Alphonse, captain of the Walloon Guard, in service to the king of Spain, making his way north to Madrid. For two entire months, some eight hundred pages, he keeps winding along through the wilds of the Sierra Morena, what was supposed to be the shortest route to the capital. We might say he's lost, or delusional, or spinning a yarn. A desert mystic; a ghost whisperer. He doesn't belong there, even if somehow the rest of them do—the seductive sister princesses of Moorish lineage also known as his cousins, the hermit priest, the Kabbalist and his erudite sister, the head of the gypsies (*bohémiens*), Velasquez the geometer. Where else could he be but Spain? Less the teller than the collector of tales, juggler of other tellers. Doesn't belong, as his attendant well knows: "Officers of the Walloon Guard were heretics, you could tell by their blond hair, blue eyes, red cheeks." And yet there he is, ever the stranger, hearing them out.

In the movie, naturally, Alphie is Polish, I mean the

actor is Polish, young and brave and stumbling into fantastic situations, he can't believe his luck. As much a project of cultural reclamation, the film adds a further layer of amusement, to see those Polish faces transformed as ostensibly Spanish characters in their full range— the princesses, the priest, the Kabbalist, his sister. They might very well be in Poland! The lead actor who died too soon, like his counterpart in America, restless spirits both, bewigged and beclothed in the period uniform of a gentleman and military officer, out of this world. Journey quests, unexpected esoteric wisdom; transits of philosophical, ethno-historical inquiry. Did the actors realize what they were in the middle of? Or were they just having fun, buoyed up on sparks of divine laughter? The Polish rider, our Alphonse: and where was he going? Was the Walloon Guard just waiting around for him to get there?

Presumably those Walloons, with their captain, would be speaking French—whenever he reaches Madrid. The Spanish king and his entourage likely communicated in their own tongue to the Guard. Sure, what difference does it make except for the lovely possibilities of misunderstanding. Didn't the others encountered in the

Sierra Morena talk in Spanish? It seems the manuscript that was found in Saragossa recounting those adventures was written in the language of the land and later translated, thus perhaps not composed by the gentleman rider. Even so, the movie is in Polish, drawn from Polish sources, and Alphonse is already Alfonso. How confused was this Van Worden? Better yet, the movie was made in 1965, based on the Polish translation of 1847, a version cobbled together from available fragments. That reconstruction further elaborated, with some portions translated back from the Polish, did not appear in French until 1989 (the first more or less complete edition in its original language, though mistakenly assembled); so when another movie was made less than a decade after the first—for French television, longer and in four parts—it was taken from the only modern edition in France, a mere subset of the tales that was published in 1958, casting a different angle on Alphonse and what he found. The full expansive nature of the enterprise that was the *Manuscrit trouvé à Saragosse* could not really be appreciated, it turned out, until the scholars François Rosset and Dominique Triaire came along and found additional manuscripts, to determine that there were, in fact, three versions conceived by its author: a partial effort in the 1790s; a more ambitious take begun in 1804 and abandoned after the Forty-fifth Day; and a substantially revamped version started in 1810 and completed with the Sixty-first Day, not long before the author's suicide at home in Podolia in December 1815 at age fifty-four. The second and third versions, in their edition, came out in 2006. Less than half the tales were published in the author's lifetime, but enough to be stolen whole cloth on several occasions over the next fifty years. Alphonse, if he were paying attention, must surely have suffered an identity crisis.

Whoever he is, through the desolate heights and valleys where there always manages to be found a little wine, Alphonse remains true to his code of honor, faithful to his word as a gentleman. Even the Inquisition recognizes that he does not belong there. Still, he is invited into everyone's abode, honored guest, entertained and hosted. Captain without a company yet, cast through a *mise en abîme* of tales and interruptions along his way; or not along his way except by diversion. If he is not quite turning circles, or scared off by ghosts and demons, neither does he seem to be going in a forward direction exactly, in any case it's hard to tell. The straight line dissolves before our eyes, and the gallant horseman keeps riding.

For twenty-plus years the captain of the Walloon Guard occupied the Polish aristocrat's imagination, riding where the writer rode, far and wide. Potocki spent three months visiting Spain in the spring of 1791, Madrid through Andalucía, before moving on to visit Morocco. In subsequent decades he traveled all over central and eastern Europe, Russia, and Asia, though not to the Iberian Peninsula again. Did Alphonse lead him back there, as through dreams, or did the honorable captain, albeit a foreign hire, emerge from the landscape unbidden, quiet companion to the incomparable bookman? The author of the *Manuscrit*, insatiable in his learning and curiosity about the world, penned numerous works of history, cultural anthropology, geography, linguistics, travel reportage, studies of antiquity; he led an active life, knew people at the highest levels of literature, politics, society, science, was married twice and had five kids; yet, throughout those twenty-plus years after the visits to Spain and Morocco, in the midst of so many other places, projects, and people, Alphonse stayed in his thoughts, distilling some measure of his voluminous travels into the tales upon tales that the gallant captain becomes infused with in the course of all those Days. His Spanish Days, as the author referred to them.

My Old Room

On the surface, it would seem my old room couldn't be more familiar a place. I could walk in there right now and know just where I am. Except, no; apparently not. At what point does my old room become somewhere else? Somewhere from another time, or outside of time, its very existence rendered questionable by the revisionary force of memories.

My old room: each of us is certain we know what that is, for a while. The specificity, the warmth, the refuge. As the context filters in—the house the room was a part of, the family or other characters who lived there, the locale, the time period—the thought of that room begins to waver beneath the cascade of moments when it could be thus identified. A real place with unsuspected limits, which turned into an imagined place when we weren't looking.

For me somehow, that room still exists. A wooden box with windows and a sliding glass door looking out from the Berkeley hills toward the bay. I lived there from late high school in 1971—when my parents bought the new, all wood, split-level house—through my university years, six years in all. Over the four-plus decades since, I have visited many times and my old room is where I, or we, always stay. My mother at almost 99 still lives in the bedroom upstairs, above what was my own, her room as on a promontory pulling in all available light even on foggy mornings; the room where my father died four years ago. Where I slept, on the other hand, perched more among the trees and with a closer angle on the rooftops and gardens downhill, was a room left unpainted, nothing but planks of knotty pine all around.

Any trace of the teenager who lived within those walls is long gone. Just a few lingering details: a shelf of books and records, and a cardboard wall plate for the light switch with a bright cartoon image of The Beatles from *Yellow Submarine*. The desk and chair are the same from back then, of modern Danish design, but they don't show the years I sat there. In the corners, a few small musical instruments remain that my parents brought back for me from their trips. On the wall by the desk, which my mother has used ever since I moved out, hang various mementos of the family through subsequent periods, including a flyer from 1986 of a poetry performance I was part of at a museum in Paris and a photo twenty years later of my son, as a boy, climbing on my shoulders in our kitchen in Brooklyn.

All the same, it is a little unsettling going back to my old room. Familiar as it feels with its wood and light and sky, it reminds me that is not my place anymore. I made my life far away. So, despite our shared history, each time I return the room seems to ask: and who are you again? I would be hard pressed to answer, as if glancing in the mirror for confirmation I saw images of my face from earlier periods superimposed at random. But I'm forgetting that a face doesn't really tell the *who* of a person, any more than a room does, one's own room, and of course they both do plenty, though beware of interpreters. Only by good fortune do I still have access to that place so many years later, and especially thanks to my parents' longevity. Yet, where does it take me when I come to visit? Will I know how to leave again?

On Specs

As an object of human invention, it couldn't be more elemental, dating from ancient times: two lozenges of glass, held in place by an armature of metal or wood or other material. And the technology for producing the device has only continued to progress ever since, fine-tuning its nimble possibilities. So habituated are most people to wearing them that eyeglasses may seem a part of one's face; on some faces, we only notice when the glasses are taken off. A contraption dreamed up by science and art both, grafted onto the very person—identity conditioned by a pair of specs. Face pushed up against the window; do we have any choice if we want to see well? The glass assimilated to the eyes in their mineral embrace. Removed by the hand, it becomes an object again, external to us, no part of our blood or bone.

When I was thirteen, though, I just liked how eyeglasses looked on the face. My sister had a pair of round, gold wire frames she wasn't using anymore, so I had them fitted with plain glass and for months I wore them to school. In the photo from our eighth-grade class trip to Washington D.C. there they are, a slight gleam around my eyes. Classmates didn't know what to make of my little disguise at first, was I playing at something, and then they forgot about it. Regardless, that brief adventure wasn't anything complicated, I simply wanted to try it out for a while, that look of wearing specs. Like someone who puts on a hat when it's not for warmth or shade, as an accessory for confronting the world, even having fun with it. I don't recall why I stopped with the glasses, probably I got tired of them, the novelty wore off. That was the privilege of the matter, I could drop them when the season changed, and go back more or less to how I was.

Would that it were always so. We age, do we not? Certainly the eyes do, so much wear and tear, the elements, infinite reading. The day came, years overdue, that I had no choice but to get glasses if I wished to keep on reading. Of course, I was expecting the verdict, though when it came to selecting frames I realized I had no idea what I wanted, or almost no idea. I had never lingered much at the mirror, and I did not like having to think about how did I look with each pair of frames. After trying ten or fifteen pairs, with still more drawers of samples unexamined, the mind reeling if not for my wife—who patiently limited the choices, narrowing them down until suddenly it was obvious which were the right frames for my face, for the eyes looking out through them. There was no playing around anymore; these were yours, buddy, get used to them. I had entered the age of appendage, and I only wondered where it would stop. Or maybe I didn't wonder, I tried not to.

For years, I made an uneasy peace with my glasses, all the putting on and taking off, placing them carefully in their case that I always made room for, in pocket or bag, when I went anywhere. They had become indispensable, like a wallet and keys and money. Even so, I remained ever wary of their perfidy, as if they were secretly plotting my imminent blindness. Hadn't various people told me, when I first got my reading glasses, that my eyesight would only get worse with them? And hadn't that come to pass, as proven by each new eye exam? These interlopers on my face, who were they working for really? I admit it was nice getting the occasional compliment on the frames I had chosen—lucky I didn't know it was a designer brand before deciding on them—and my son even liked how they enhanced the Serious Writer look. Besides, the small quasi-ritual in donning them was rather enjoyable— withdrawing and opening the case, lifting out the glasses, sizing up what lay before me as I got down to business preparing to read. The frames stayed the same with each stronger prescription, and when the time came for me to yield to the imperative for distance glasses as well, I settled for more purposeful, cheaper frames, as if to set them apart. I didn't expect to use those glasses much, just for the theater and other events with my wife, though I often forgot them at home or didn't want to carry two cases with me.

Maybe because I was past fifty before I got my first prescription, on some level I've resisted glasses ever since. Sure, I see better when I have them on, but I don't want to get too used to them. And then two years ago it was inevitable, near and far converged, I got progressive lenses. Same frames. After a certain experience with them now, I can say that I'm not wild about the arrangement. I didn't understand at first why they kept saying I should get new reading glasses as well, stronger still but also not uniform, bit of a stigma in one eye. Somehow I thought the whole point of progressive lenses was one pair for everything, but these are not so great for reading, too small a part of the lens is given over to that function. So, more than ever I'm with the two pairs of glasses, determining before every move whether I need one or the other or both. Will the doctor tell me the next time I need glasses to sleep in, too? I do without either of them as often as I can manage, perhaps more than I should, for it does no good to imagine that my glasses will do all my seeing for me. They have to know their place, even when gripping the sides of my head; home is in their case, nowhere else. We will never get along completely, it took me years to understand. They may be an ancient contraption, developed to a high degree of precision, but I'm just an old skeptic. Certain kinds of seeing are simply beyond them, that's what I'm after.

While on a Mountainside in Oaxaca

How could such essential information have escaped me for so long? Or maybe it was not essential, in the here and now, for an American kid growing up in the sixties, whose grandparents were all immigrants and didn't live nearby. Raised on American TV and American comic books and Anglo-American pop music, I was hardly aware that the world existed in anything but English. If I knew something of Hebrew, it was because our family used to go to *shul* and because my brother and sister and finally me, we all went to Hillel School for our education. Yiddish, to me, was more a remnant, heard in words and phrases exchanged by my parents with their families, and others at *shul*, though never much. More dynamically, Yiddish was the past and no one around me dwelled on the past, especially in what that entailed of an old world. And if I was at all conscious as a kid of the Spanish language, it was mostly because of Mexican food, which my family never ate. Besides, wasn't it the tendency of most immigrants in America to leave the old tongue behind, not pass it down? Somehow there were no circumstances for me to have learned such details about my parents, not till I was seventeen, as it happened.

One day in the summer of 1973, Isaac and his cousin

Nicky and I were trying psilocybin mushrooms on a mountainside in Oaxaca, while hundreds of miles away in Puebla a terrible earthquake occurred. Of course, when we eventually found out about it, we had no thoughts to call home, which would have been complicated. My parents, living in Berkeley by then, only knew we were traveling in Mexico somewhere. Weeks later, I discovered that my father, seeking to know more, had gotten on the phone and called Isaac's house in Chula Vista and landed on his Polish grandfather, who had immigrated to Mexico in the 1920s. Isaac's grandfather spoke little English, and my father's Spanish was nil, but apparently they figured out they had recourse to the old lingua franca. Before that, I had no idea my father was so fluent in Yiddish.

ACHES AND PAINS

The aches and pains of returning to the gym after a month away—as if my body had forgotten, or tried to forget, the rigors of exercise. The use it or lose it school, muscles' memory interrupted, reflexes diverted by travel or national holidays or weather events. What seems clear is my body does not feel as it did, when it's been put through the paces, and I hadn't noticed the changes occur.

Is it still my body?

I know by experience that it will change again and yet again, and that all is not lost, agility and strength can still be regained, with regular effort. Those pains will be forgotten too; which hardly seems possible until it happens, just when you thought you knew your body by its pains. But that was illusion, a map for the mind. Doesn't our body continue to surprise us with its developments?

It would be hard to say, in fact, which is my real body. At what moment?

The body we recognize as our own: we are glad to not have to think about it, to take it for granted, as though we expected to always be able to walk along as we walk today.

But the lingering image lags behind us, I'm afraid. Our material selves keep finessing their impertinent adjustments, each day closer to a secret resolution, while we seek only to cloak ourselves in reason and righteous visions.

Talking to Strangers

Five days east to west and back, crisscrossing the country: the difference was dramatic if you glanced around. At first, the signs were almost pleasantly disturbing. Yesterday, the 26th of February at San Francisco Airport, hardly anyone was in front of me going through security; at the gate, plenty of places to sit could be found even up till boarding. It only hit me after we'd already been flying a couple hours and I went to the bathroom in mid cabin—gazing back the way I came, I saw rows upon rows of empty seats staring me in the face. My own row was completely full, though I hadn't exchanged a word with anyone. I thought I might share my observation when I got back to my seat, with the couple on the inside beside me, but the occasion didn't present itself. A while later, I got up to let them out and made my remark then, and they too were surprised. Standing in the aisle, I noticed a sprawling crowd of lit screens on the seats ahead all tuned to the home page of the entertainment system, unmoving. I had just finished watching Hitchcock's *Foreign Correspondent*, which started before the plane took off; I realized I'd never seen it before. Nor had I ever seen a plane half empty.

Welcome to the latest human contagion, the new

coronavirus leaping across the planet. It was serious a week ago, of course, but in the days since it has spread further still while the stock market plunged precipitously. On the flight out of New York last week, full as usual, I spent the first half hour talking with the woman seated next to me, whom I'd helped to stow her coat. She was a lawyer, fortyish, studying for an exam she was going to take in Oakland. Originally from India, she had lived in New York since college, with some time in London before that, I think. In the course of discussing such movements and where one lives, I told her that all my grandparents were immigrants and some had even settled in Oakland. We could have gone on talking amiably, but I wanted to let her get back to her studying and I also looked forward to whatever I might decide on for entertainment. Nobody flies in a plane to embark on a conversation, but wedged into our seats like that sometimes it happens anyway.

A few years ago, my wife and I were flying to Paris, I was in the middle seat, and a young woman sat in the aisle beside me; as she settled her several parcels, I noticed she was wearing a head scarf. In a short time—I don't recall how she started talking with us, but casually enough—we learned she had come from New Mexico and was on her way to Algeria to see her husband and live with him a while among his family. She would go back to New Mexico eventually with him, where she had most of her own family. They had met through the internet, and this was only the third or fourth time she would be with him. Naturally she was carrying various gifts and supplies for her hosts. Each new element of her story had me wondering how in the world was it possible, such turns in a life. She spoke happily about her comings and goings, and with almost the same sense of wonder.

All children are told not to talk to strangers, and for good reason, but out of need or curiosity at some point early on we ignore that injunction and venture forth. It is not an easy thing, talking to strangers, always to invite the unexpected. Traveling in close quarters for long distances, we're bound to have some exchange with other passengers. And sometimes, that determines what comes next. When I was nineteen, with two college friends I took a bus from Tijuana to Mexico City, forty-six hours. Somewhere en route we got to speaking with two guys in the seats across who lived in the capital, in the end they let us stay at their apartment. From there, two of us met other people whom we each stayed with longer—me in

Tlatelolco for a month and a half with ten engineering students from Aguascalientes—while the third returned to California since our original plan to continue south had evidently gotten derailed. Because of those conversations on the bus; and days later, because of other conversations in Chapultepec Park. On the other hand, you don't even have to speak up in the right conditions. That same trip, I was sitting on a step one day by the Tlatelolco metro station and reading a small, cheap edition I'd bought at a kiosk, of Neruda's *Veinte poemas de amor*. No sooner did a student come striding out of the station, he stooped to see the title of my book and went off declaiming one of the poems by heart.

Salutary as such encounters may be, we can't just go out and start talking to strangers left and right. Eventually we'd be locked up, public nuisance. These are delicate matters.

And now, six weeks later, we're locked up the whole day long at home. We may as well yearn for those bygone days when we could strike up a conversation like that with someone we'd never seen before just because we happened to be seated beside each other, breathing the same air for a spell.

Before Our Eyes

How fragile is the familiar world we inhabit, it turns out (although we always knew). Glance away at the wrong moment—and the tenuous threads holding it all together snap, what appeared so firm becomes undone. Surely it is better to forget than to live in constant anticipation of the event, for catastrophe stalks our every step. To look back is to be amazed we are still here, survivors of our own recklessness; or of our own good luck.

A letter writer to the *New York Times*, last week, understands how to live with that breach stretching out unsuspected beside us: "When I see someone homeless, I not only give something but I also try to talk to the person. Once, a friend who was with me asked why. It was because that person's eyes were mine. The fear and confusion were mine. The sense of helplessness and sometimes hopelessness were mine. The looking up from such a bleak place had been mine more than once…" (Stewart Frimer, Forest Hills, Queens, "The Look of Empathy," 29 April 2020). Of course, we shouldn't have to have *been there* to recognize the situation, there but for fortune and all. Every religion teaches as much, and yet so-called "people of faith" are no better at basic humanity than the rest of us. Probably most people want to be good, or to be seen as good, none of that really counts. The gods will sort it out if they are able, but we must answer to ourselves.

However much we try to forget, in order to get on with our lives, like it or not the fact is we also remember. If we live in an American city, the reminders are everywhere and we don't even have to make the obvious connections: ever more skyscrapers, the growing heaps of luxury goods, unstoppable gentrification, the preciousness and commodification of formerly simple pleasures; and in the wake of all that razzle dazzle, washed ashore and stranded along the same sidewalks where satisfied shoppers carry home their latest prizes, those who could not keep up with the rising costs of life. So dire is this state of affairs, and so seemingly bereft of solutions, that we reluctantly accept it; merely to describe it comes off as old news. What else can we do? An entire population left to sink away in plain sight, let them go, cast outside our human ken. Ever since the reign of Saint Reagan, America has been bent on manufacturing the homeless, a real growth industry. But we can say a prayer for them.

Surely the reflex to not see is nothing new, nor limited

to the self-described greatest country in the world. The old and infirm, who would be more inconvenient to the smooth functioning of our daily existence, at least can be looked after in one of the many thousands of institutions throughout the land. That is, if the funds can be coaxed forth from some ready pocket, there is a place where they may wait out their remaining days, away from us. Whether such homes retain enough trained personnel, or adequate supplies and space, or a budget to properly accommodate lives not yet spent entirely, the new customers handing over their loved one for storage must go on some measure of trust, once the cheery salespeople and publicity brochures have prepared the ground. Even with visits and a curiosity to glimpse how the time passes there, we do not want to know too much; as it is, we barely escaped with our own skins. Contrary to the homeless, pushed out yet somehow persistently present, the residents of these homes, who fade with the passing months, will never leave there except one way.

But we want what's best for them, don't we? Just as we do for the nation's war veterans who fought so valiantly on our behalf and lost their wits or limbs or lesser parts in the full glory of that warmaking and for which we honor them—once or twice a year's not too much to ask—by waving a flag or dropping a dollar in the cup or muttering a magic formula that might sooner translate as "better them than us." Or maybe they were truly lucky, and suffered no discernible loss, nor trauma from what they saw. Let us not dwell on the criminality of wars, or that those who go off to battle as part of something greater than themselves are usually recruited on false pretenses. The veterans who move among us in America bear a secret mark that the rest of us can barely fathom: confirmation of war's futility, its pure waste, even if they themselves believe no such thing. The nation, to the degree there is one, will never make it. up to them, and they know that.

How can we carry on as if nothing mattered beyond our front door? It's only a door, after all. In the midst of the coronavirus pandemic, recently, it was revealed at a veterans' home in Holyoke, Massachusetts, that some seventy veterans had died from the virus, the most at any such facility up till then. Understaffed and overcrowded, like many others. Did no one have a clue before it was too late? And what could they have done? Life tends to be more complicated than it has to be, and most often we just end up struggling through the confusion. Ghosts are everywhere about us, and we cannot bring ourselves to look them in the eye. Or else, it's the other way around. Maybe I am the ghost, and they the keepers of this broken world?

In the Fields of Unknowing

Amid all the startling dissonance in this sudden new time that humankind is living through, from our extended period of confinement that promises to stretch on and on well beyond any semblance of reopening, the proliferation of hours spent before our screens strikes a curious resonance with an ancient allegory. The confinement is relative, its degree dependent on dictates of the state or localities; and whatever the dictates, the need to avoid contagion will remain paramount. But to call ourselves prisoners misses the mark significantly. We are still free to go out and shop for food, even to take a walk, in many places, as long as we don't congregate with others in close proximity (though political urgency supersedes self-isolating). So, we are confined to private spaces mostly, and thus somehow to more of a private mind as well (the truly essential workers in our societies, by contrast, are thrust into quite the opposite predicament, with only the slightest margins in which to think of their own safety). Our screens, therefore, offer not just comfort and escape, but also confirmation of what we left behind, what awaits us, what is stirring even now *out there somewhere*. These images, we are convinced, are more real than mere shadows on the wall.

At the same time, our distance from those images—which is also the function of a screen, an instrument of distancing that both keeps out and lets in—casts a vein of doubt through our sense of what we're seeing. Can things really be like that? Could they not have changed since those images were sent? Or, we warm to them precisely because we know they are from another time, almost within reach, but not quite. The screen is a form of theater even when the transmission is direct, in the moment, even where the premise is that this is not a performance. Fantasy or document, or simple two-way communication, we must nonetheless play along. You are there, the screens insist. We have to believe in the images, or else we are lost; the foundations of what we take for reality depend on it, so any doubts are kept at bay. Like the howling of coyotes at the edge of our hearing, those doubts are effectively screened out. As the sheen of certainty settles over us, we can close our eyes again, go back to sleep, secure in what we'll find on waking.

The shadows may be fleshed out as images on our screens, with the appearance of dimension and even biographies, but they remain projections. We are drawn along by their spell and would prefer never to question their hold on us, were it not for that restlessness that would have us sour on paradise itself given the chance. Told to stay cloistered, to hang tight with what we have, sooner or later one of us will break out, probably many, simply to prove they can, that some half-baked spirit of independence might yet be summoned. Will they recognize what they're looking at, discern any difference? The buildings are still there, the trees, the squirrels; other people appear much the same, albeit fewer, the streets less busy. So, the screens didn't lie, the widely touted new normal failed to materialize. Those who ventured out did not have to adjust their sight after all, it seems; they saw what they expected. The vanished world stands before us, imposing as ever, vanishing from within because we were too distracted by all the pretty surfaces. Can it be that so many screens led us to forget how to see with more than our eyes?

But here, in this allegory of the screens, a cracked allegory where nothing keeps its place, a great many of us understood from the moment we got stuck inside that those surfaces were in fact transparent. As we long suspected, the reality we took as unassailable turned out to be an accretion of our bad habits, our desires and denials, our petty pretensions and pieties. Solace in traditions can only take us so far. There outside, in the fields of our unknowing, we can yet learn where it is we need to go.

Outs and Ins

You too can become an insider (unless you're already there; in which case, don't move). You too can be a member of the club (with all the benefits that may confer: initiating conspiracies; towel service; fellow members to vouch for you). Don't forget to sneer at everyone left out, they were never going to make it anyhow, who were they kidding? You simply have no time for them now, that's the way it is. Surely it's a mark of your intelligence, your good breeding, your superior instincts to be in the know, at the center of where things are happening. Those who count recognize as much. But what if, one day, your infallible antennae dropped the signal?

In this year of the raging virus, the challenge is especially acute. Most of us do all we can to stay at home, out of harm's way, careful not to get infected. If we managed to get through the early months oblivious to the dangers, better not to tiptoe too near the edge once we're more informed. We may even be blessed that no one close has succumbed, far as we're aware, though some have told us they got sick, the misery and pain, before their gradual recovery. Did a stroke of bad luck just catch up with them? What special powers were they endowed with as a result of pulling through? And no lingering damage? One old friend tells me of another friend, a hypochondriac in the best of times, now every day he's announcing symptoms. He must have fallen ill ten times over, and yet he stands. The club with the desirable antibodies will not take him. Or look at others, not deemed essential workers and having no cause to cast their profile against the future dawn, who must nonetheless hurl themselves past the jaws of death, for the times demand nothing less. But if it's merely glory they seek, make room for disappointment: there is no club for heroes.

No doubt the fear of missing out has always existed, at least to a minor degree. Isn't that why some people moved to certain cities? Quite understandable when you live in what comes to feel like a dead zone. Life inevitably seems to be elsewhere. In recent years, however, the phrase has gained such currency, thanks to social media, that it is reduced to its initials and even cited as a four-letter acronym in op-ed pieces in major newspapers. Thus, one has to be in the know enough to decipher the odd-looking abbreviation; what may at first sound like a foreign term, or a choice bit of hip slang, confirms in turn (once you've caught on) that you're not so dumb after all.

The gesture, the desire, the lack made manifest by that fear suggests an imbalance that will not easily be resolved. The dictates of fashion, in whatever domain, have grown so fierce that its followers are left in a perpetual state of insecurity; their fleeting moments of contentment last hardly longer than the snapshot that shows they were there, in a scripted place they could never find on their own. Rest assured there is a vast battalion of middlemen to help you along to the next happy place, carefully appointed with all the right accessories to prove you haven't lost your touch, your flair, your impeccable taste, who cares if it isn't really yours, everything fits just like the magazine said it should. The influencers and critics, the curators and experts do all the knowing for you, no contract required, you can trust them, that's what they are paid to do. They have a knack for that sort of thing, their nose on the pulse, finger to the wind; they've put their time in the trenches. Besides, it can be such a bore figuring it out for yourself, with the roundabout moves and the time wasted and looking like a fool. There are too many books, and movies, and plays, and TV shows, too many music and dance performances, plus museum exhibits, galleries, and all those other events, it's so bewildering, let alone telling the difference between what you like and what you should like. Some guidance, please. Or maybe start with the basics: which sublime or edgy food spot should you make an expedition to, what's the chef's pedigree, or where is the one place you must absolutely put in an appearance, costs be damned? Depends whose advice you seek, of course, that's why the gods invented research. But who has the energy to keep up?

Still, you don't want to miss out. If it's history in the making, you ought to try to be there. Staying tuned to the latest buzz wasn't meant to be easy, the demands are relentless. One must have a flexible neck and well-greased eyeballs, like that person you thought you were having a conversation with who doesn't stop glancing about the room in case someone more important to talk to comes along. Take a page from them, they might know something. It's all well and good to be a sophisticate in the big city, but you can always slip up, mention a name that no one takes seriously, wear the wrong ridiculous hat, and like that reveal your bumpkin nature for everybody to see. Study and learn, even if you're from that very same city, you must study and learn what others do, and not be too original, eccentric perhaps, just don't let them doubt you belong.

On the other hand, there remains an alternate route to gaining your place among the cool kids, one that's packed with more adventure and a shiver of danger. Wave the flag of Rimbaud or Burroughs—or take your pick, there's probably a list somewhere—pledge the no-allegiance, click your boots three times, and you just might find yourself enfolded in the camp of renegades and outlaws. That doesn't mean you'll be banished forever from the hallowed halls, only that you might have to make some noise a while, and dance your renegade dance, wear your outlaw pants, before they locate your name tag. You can be as much an outsider as you like, go on, strike up the pose, heaps of scorn, hold it. Hold. Good, now come in and get your supper. If you breathe fire and show some independence, it might take a little longer but that just ups your profile. Forget about being left out. The bad boys and girls get their own special seats, one never knows what they might do or say in polite company. You will be part of what others don't want to miss.

POLISH THING

Me them? How did it not occur to me until I was around thirty that I'm also Polish?

The explanation is easy enough: for Jews in America, it has to do with *last known origin*. I grew up hearing that my mother's parents were Russian Jews when they immigrated, and my father's were Austro-Hungarian. As a kid, somehow I never thought to ask my grandparents, when I saw them once or twice a year, about the old country. The whole idea seemed unimaginably remote. Those places, as we knew, did not exist anymore. Of course, where they were from depended on when they left. And only as an adult did I begin to understand how that played out.

Somewhere along the line—because I asked?—I learned that my mother's parents came from the vicinity of Bialystok. That's clearly in eastern Poland, but before World War I it flew a different flag. My father's mother, who died before I was born, was a Galitzianer, around Krakow, I think. Until she emigrated, after the war, that was the previous empire. Poland wasn't what they knew.

The connections were buried in plain sight. But what does it matter where my ancestors kicked up dust? Even if, for all I know, they remained in that locale for hundreds of years, regardless of the shift in borders, in ruling powers, in the prevailing tongue. How do any such details affect that box of tricks we call identity?

The biographical coordinates aside, from my university years on and not for any discernible reason or purpose I developed a growing curiosity about things Polish, or Polish-related, mostly through music and literature, but also film, politics, history, people. The klezmer revival was first going strong back then in the seventies, on the west coast and the east; that helped draw my attention to that general part of Europe. In the school library, I chanced on a new anthology of Polish avant-garde theater, Witkiewicz and others. Within a few years, I became aware of early Polanski and Wajda, and the great living poets, and earlier modernists Bruno Schultz and Gombrowicz, also the journalist Kapuscinski (my craze for Potocki and Komeda came later). What's more, I started contributing jazz reportage to a journal edited in Warsaw. And Solidarnosc burst out of nowhere too, in that time. At some point amid those various starbursts of consciousness, I heard Poland described as the Latin America of Europe and that caught my ear, made me think about parallels: their long sufferings at the hands of dominant powers, which possibly explained their over-the-top embrace of the Jewish hippie king; but also the wild imagination, their energy. The comparison helped reinforce my affinity for whatever this was known as Poland.

One time I came close to studying the language. I acquired a set of instructional tapes and a small dictionary. Or rather, the tapes were after and the dictionary before the only trip I made there. Seven years I'd been sending articles to *Jazz Forum*, which published an international edition in English, and each fall they would ask if I was going to attend the Jazz Jamboree, the big festival that had been going for three decades. Finally, I said yes and booked my ticket to Warsaw. By then, I knew more or less where my grandparents had come from, but that didn't fit into my plans: I had no personal references to seek out there. Even so, the trip was filled with stimulating encounters, and still I didn't make much effort with those language tapes.

If culturally I have some kind of elusive bond with Poland, however distant, that sympathy or reflex predates any knowledge of biographical facts. How is it that so many works and figures that have fascinated me over the years happen to be Polish? I would be hard-pressed to identify a particular essence common to them all; and yet. As if every last one stood at the edge of hallucination, like their Latin American cousins. Where the world never ceases to act strangely, and most often in a darkly comic way.

A land, a country, whose borders changed many times through the centuries: Poland wobbles in place. By the time I had kids, I began to wonder if there might even be room for me. Was it possible to obtain dual citizenship? The idea was, Polish papers would thereby grant me a European Union passport, and that status should ultimately pass on to my kids, so I hoped. My eligibility was premised on having grandparents born near Bialystok. The whole process seemed pretty standard, following Ireland's practice since at least the eighties when I heard about it; as a later member of the European Union, maybe Poland adopted a similar policy. I had it all worked out very nicely in my head—which is where it remained, since I wasn't able to locate any birth records for my grandparents, nor did I get around to ascertaining whether such a policy actually existed, that might have been pure speculation on my part.

At the end of my marvelous journey to Warsaw and

Krakow and points south to Zakopane, in the weeks of October-November 1987, I visited a state-run book and record shop in Warsaw (where I also bought a couple of lovely woven floor runners). I found a big art book on Witkacy (Witkiewicz), a lot of his painting and photography experiments between the wars, text in Polish. And I selected a boxful of vinyl, everything very cheap at the exchange rate I was getting. I had so many carry-on parcels on the flight home, one might have thought I was emigrating. In the past week, I've brought up from the basement about half those records—the Polish productions, not the Czech or Hungarian or Russian releases. Modern composers, village folk music, classics for pipe organ, jazz. Now it's Mme. Danuta Kleczkowska, native of Lodz, on harpsichord playing a Baroque repertoire, recorded in 1980. Presumably, I listened to the album at least once in the past thirty-three years, and it's pleasant enough for what it is, no sparks, so having heard it again I can put it away for another long sleep. Not like the folk fiddling from the southeast village of Piatkowa (Subcarpathian province), those four sides are growing on me. Fiddle backed by hammered dulcimer, often a second fiddle, and sometimes a bass; mostly played by older members of the

Sowa family, in the mid-1970s. Half the tunes have vocals, and those are raw as only country music can be. Between the jaunty wedding pieces on the first side and the madcap polkas on the fourth, I am able to imagine I hear a sort of Polish duende.

So, who could lay claim to this Polish duende? Possibly anyone who has lived in those lands. And what does it consist of? Difficult to say, though a sense of humor goes a long way. Even Jews, do they partake of it? Without a doubt, after all these centuries together. Polish duende, did I make it up? It exists in every dictionary of Polish phenomena plus most annals of paranormal energy transference. Then how shall we define it? No need, inspiration takes many forms but doesn't come begging for favors.

What can we hope to glean of a heritage from past lives? It's a matter of luck and resistance if much of anything survives. There are always traces, like lines in a face or some arcane small habit, that carry messages from long ago and far away, though we no longer know how to read them. Immigrants don't look back, they shed whatever they have to. I don't speak the language, no tales of the old country were told in the family; any dreams that stalk me were cooked up by others. Besides, the places aren't what they were, every possible connection washed clean. It is easy to imagine, after all, in Brooklyn I could walk down the street one day and pass someone who happens to be a direct descendant of the people who lived across from my great-grandparents in that village near Bialystok, and I wouldn't have the slightest notion. We are walking memories unaware of ourselves, radiating our many instances of belonging and not belonging as we move through the world, scarcely seeing what is right in front of us.

The Shape We're In

The other day in the park, a cyclist was telling her fellow cyclist as they sailed past, "I'm so out of shape!" What is this shape that people have in mind when they say that? Well, we all know, sort of: it's a vague thing, a way of imagining our best physical self, most vitality, lightness and strength, where perhaps for a moment or a long while we once held steady. It may be that the mirror bears some reflection of that shape, out or in, but when we're not looking, which is most often, the measure comes more from the inside, how we feel in our body. That way, the ideal is when we're not feeling much of anything: no creakiness, no great effort in movement, no fatigue. Our body's silence, as it were, seems like confirmation that we're doing just fine. The body's always joking, of course; plays fast and loose; and just when we take it for granted, like any other organism or machine, surprise.

The shape we're in, good or bad, inevitably carries some grain of disappointment. After all that, it comes to this? Some other person's shape is how we see our own. So many bodies to choose from, and attitudes. The whole long way through life, we model ourselves on what we see and know, that is our reflecting pool. I don't mean looking at tall people all day will make me taller, would be interesting; rather, how people stand or sit, how they walk across the room, how they move their arms, how they occupy space, so many such details register in us unaware. Other people's behavior affects how we behave, naturally enough, even at a distance, while it also shows the capacities of our resistance. That resistance shapes us more than anything, tells who we are amid all the cross-traffic.

No two shapes alike, should be the warning. Said another way: there is only the one shape that fits each of us alone in all our particulars, now as then, now as will be. The aspirational shape we might yet get into resides in us already; it will emerge one day soon. In the meantime—keep digging.

SECONDHAND

The charm of used objects, though acquired for their attractive price, is that they carry a life with them already. For some things that's all right, and likely we take no interest in their history except for the company they provide. The breath and attention spent over them by previous owners, however fleeting, nameless, still radiates in their thick skins. Used furniture, used clothes and decorations: legacy of strangers passing in the night.

Books all the more so. We buy a book used simply because it's cheaper or it can't be found new, and we accept because what can you do that others had it in their hands before we did. Even so, we'd prefer the book have no markings in it, no trace of its past. But you can't always get that and then you ignore the scrawl in the margin, the underlining, the name written inside the cover that you refuse to remember. We do not want to know if someone read our copy, or what they thought of it, or whether their house was happy or sad. Even if we could find our way back to them, as though to climb up the stream of ownership, we are not welcome there. Yet, who were they?

The name found inside the cover, it's a lie. Maybe it was true once, but that person doesn't live here now.

You yourself would never think to write your name in a book like that, where would it end—unless it's just for books you were going to let loose in the world. On the other hand, that name inscribed on the flyleaf may be of someone you knew or had a connection to. Your mother, your grandfather. In which case, the book itself becomes invested with marvelous properties. Any number of scenarios spring to mind, casting light on the volume you're holding and its former owner. Here they are, sharing something with you.

A different signature, often on the title page, poses a challenge of another sort. When the author signs their book for you, presumably yours is a new copy; regardless, then and there it becomes used, saddled with a past. That handwritten mark among the printed pages binds you almost, as to promise this book personally signed shall remain in your collection forevermore. The signature adds value, but above all it brings us closer to the person who dreamed up that book. Their hands have touched these pages.

It doesn't seem right, therefore, browsing in a secondhand bookshop, to chance upon a signed copy on the shelves. The reader let the writer down, it would seem.

You're not supposed to sell those books; signed editions are for keeping. How did it end up here? Worse yet if there's a dedication, with a name, so we can see who betrayed the writer's gift. It's embarrassing to witness, like we should turn and walk away; instead, we consider buying it, at that price. The record of their lapsed exchange, between writer and friend, makes for a most particular copy, extra features for the curious collector.

The errant signature, ever more and less a part of the book, may prove to be a wild card, an independent element that can affect the whole enterprise. What is to be done, though, with a secondhand signature, where the dedication has been negated by circumstances? That's tricky business when the copy remains in the author's possession. One old friend, who has signed many of her books to me, turned the situation to advantage once when she gave me a copy she had just signed to someone else the day before, which for whatever reason did not go to them. I had recently gotten married, so the new note, addressed to me and my wife, referred to the double dedication and how that bodes well, according to the Chinese, for love and happiness. I did not pass a similar test with such grace. For some time, I'd been occasionally buying used copies of my first book, which was long out of print yet fairly cheap online, to have on hand to give away when I felt like it. Inevitably one copy I received was a book I'd signed many years ago. The recipient was a fellow translator I'd never met but corresponded with at various points. Was she downsizing? Did she die? (I only learned just now that she did, and that she was also much older than me.) When I gave it to I don't remember who, clearly a used copy, my second dedication made no mention of the first.

More unsettling still, in the annals of runaway signatures, I was visiting friends in an old university town and they took me to a used bookstore that was a classic of its kind: upstairs, a bit dusty, with row after row of poorly marked shelves. A place to get buried in if you weren't careful. I had no intention of finding anything, but I did have to make some effort. We were about to finish up when we found ourselves before a set of smaller shelves at the end of a row. Foreign language, other odd stuff. I peered into the mix of book spines and somehow I landed pretty quickly on a thin volume I recognized, of less than fifty pages. In fact, I had found my own copy more than thirty years earlier, when it came out, in a small bookshop in a coastal village in Spain. It had been published in

Madrid. Certainly, I was surprised to find another copy in a used bookshop in an American university town, so I took it from the shelf. I thought we shouldn't leave it there, and so I tried to convince my friend that he should buy it. Inside was a dedication which the writer—who later became a friend of mine—addressed to an eminent literary couple who lived in that town, whom he was friendly with before I knew him. I had heard they had a house filled with books. How was it possible that this slim and elegant volume, signed by a friend, could have leaped clear of their collection, exiled to that unassuming spot on the bookstore shelf? It didn't make sense to me, and I don't expect I'll ever know. My friend bought the book, ten dollars, and an hour later changed his mind, so I bought it from him as I should have done in the first place. Now I happily have two copies, and the one that's signed isn't to me.

Physical Education

Whether it is a natural law or simply my own screwball logic, I have always imagined there was a direct relation between my father being a physician (Ob-Gyn) and my general ignorance of medical matters. Notwithstanding such questions, I have learned through the years, like a drip drip drip slowly penetrating my youthful obliviousness, that we can hardly feel another person's pain—let alone the contours of their illness— if we have not experienced something comparable. Imagination will only get us so far; where that fails, compassion must do the rest, no excuses. For the longest time, beyond a few stitches and bruises, I was lucky in maintaining my physical integrity and without having to think about it too much: no internal rebellions, no fateful collisions, no black holes of the personal or public variety. Then one winter day when I was twenty-eight, on the Catalan coast, likely due to a tainted sea urchin, I came down with a case of hepatitis. Over the following days, quite unaware, I started noticing strange phenomena of the bodily sort, details one after another that I had never seen before and which did not add up to any meaning I could fathom. If my body was telling me something, I needed an interpreter, but to reach even that understanding took me at least a week.

In the meantime, I caught the night train back home to Paris, where the girlfriend I had encouraged months ago to move out, who was still there, somehow managed not to get infected. Despite her hard-earned experience of ailments, and her shaky accumulation of folk wisdom, she could not read my symptoms either. Through four and a half years in Europe I had not gone to a doctor, or perhaps once for a cold, but since it was clear that something was askew in me, I walked over to the public hospital Pitié-Salpêtrière. After waiting an hour and a half among thirty other patients, I was called in to see a doctor. No sooner did I begin to list the signs, he kicked back in his chair and with almost a laugh, it was so obvious, he told me what was wrong. The verdict sounded serious. Had I not been seated, I might have fainted. At the same time, I thought, So *that's* what hepatitis is. I had known the word since forever, without much idea what all was bound up in it. Suddenly I had a small glimpse of my own mortality. The doctor called in a nurse to take a sample of my blood. With her cigarette in one hand and a syringe in the other, she completed her task and sent me on my way.

Another revelation was that there was no medication to cure me. I had only to let my body recover through the ensuing months and avoid alcohol and rich foods. My liver had been poisoned but gradually the symptoms would subside. A less visible effect, however, wormed its way into my thinking. I am not given to depression, yet I was soon questioning what was I doing with my life. Freelance writer, more or less bohemian, contemplative, who had so far dodged any standard career path. Maybe I should do something for the benefit of society, maybe I should go to law school. I said as much to my parents when they came to visit a few months after my diagnosis, as we walked along the alley of plane trees in the Jardin des Plantes, and to my father's everlasting credit—Jewish, first generation born in America, started medical school at nineteen—he dismissed my speculations, saying that was the illness talking. To accept that someone else might be masquerading in my voice, rather than seize on the opening I provided, was a tremendous gift to me. Nonetheless, was I a changed man after the season of my infirmity? A little, not much; my reservoir of foolishness was not so easily depleted.

In the span of time that is our life, genetic and

environmental mechanisms work their secret magic to determine just how much luck we get to squander—or even, sometimes, to spend wisely. But these forces, adhering to their own clocks, inevitably surprise us at some turn. How did that happen, we ask, where did it come from? The capacity for such changes is stored within us, mysteriously unfolding as we look elsewhere. The hand becomes a claw, the eye an asteroid, the ear a trapdoor to the conversation of fishes. Who did we think we were? No matter our intentions, sooner or later our bodies get away from us and we must come to terms, broker a compromise, with our new physical order. And just as in the storybooks, it can happen overnight.

There have been a few rare instances where I spotted something on my body one day that had previously escaped my attention. How long has that been there? And, what is it? Like the ganglion cyst that showed up on my wrist, nearly thirty years ago, as if a bone were trying to poke out through my skin. Not to go all sci-fi, but was some creature starting to take over from inside? The doctor, with not the slightest sense of wonder that I brought in buckets, explained what it was and that it would probably go away on its own; which it did, eventually. So, no surprise, I was spoiled in that the few maladies to beset me were mostly conditions that would take care of themselves, let the body do its thing. When I woke up in the middle of the night not long ago, with an excruciating pain in my big toe and around the ball of my foot, naturally I preferred to think it too would soon vanish. I couldn't believe that any exercise or exertions had been so extreme as to cause damage. A week later, with my foot swollen and barely able to put on my shoe, I went to the doctor. All indications led him to conclude that I had an attack of gout. Again, a word I had known since forever without really knowing what it was. How was it possible? Whose foot was that? I ate a pretty healthy diet, I wasn't prone to excess; I didn't fit the part.

Here the learned writer might feel inclined or obliged to offer a literary tour of gout, the great scenes of indulgence and its aftermath, ultimately of a comic bent, that run through the history of literature. But if I ever read any of those books, such scenes left no trace in my memory; at best, they would have seemed from another time. When the doctor first pronounced his diagnosis, he asked if I knew the old swashbuckler *Captain Blood*, where the colonial governor keeps having to put his foot up, at every appearance, to ease his pains. Nor had I seen that film.

What struck me, though, about this new affliction in late middle age, was how easy I had it compared to my two closest longtime friends who'd been contending with far scarier health issues in recent years. Considering the matter from that angle, I well understood the privilege in my sufferings, just as I had always enjoyed a greater degree of comforts than they had.

In the past week, after two more flares of gout each a month apart, I have started taking regular medication— for the first time in my life, on the cusp of turning sixty-five. I expected the day would come, for one condition or another, though not this. Call it aging if you like, or the body's contradictions resolving themselves at their own pace, its hidden springs pushing forth unsuspected weaknesses and strengths. We lose our innocence not just once, it turns out, but over and over, sparking new revolutions of consciousness each time. Another body, our own; another language, our own; another place, a people, more sentient beings at every turn, even where we had not recognized affect or effect. Our stubbornness is legendary and still, we keep learning new tricks despite ourselves.

TROUBLE WITH THE TRIBE

In the many different communities that one will find, are there ever likely to be more dissidents, proportionately, than among Jews? The variations on identity and counter-identity are so numerous, it's a wonder one can speak of a people at all. Yet there are histories, narratives, neuroses shared, questions of belief or practice need not enter into the matter. If you want to call yourself a Jew, fine, God bless (or the spirit or extraterrestrial of your choice, or none of the above); if you would rather not mention your filiation, not wanting to get tossed too easily into a preconceived box, you don't have to, others will be happy to do that for you. Either way, the old argument comes bubbling up, familiar under other banners: But are you Jewish enough?

Long ago, when I was nineteen and staying for a month with ten engineering students from Aguascalientes in their three-bedroom apartment on the top floor of a high-rise public housing building in Tlatelolco, Mexico City, I met a guy who lived in one of the single-room bungalows up on the roof. He was about our age and at some point he took down from his shelf a blue velvet bag, ten inches square, that I vaguely recognized. With the Hebrew letters on the front, indeed it was a *tefillin* bag like I had in the year leading up to my bar-mitzvah. What an unexpected place to come upon such a thing. He had no idea what to do with phylacteries and retained them as a relic from a family past he hardly knew. Would he have gained Jew points in some rabbis' ledgers simply for keeping those ritual accessories? My own *tefillin* were long gone: I had no use for them.

Some months earlier, my first girlfriend came to visit from the Jersey shore and stayed with me at my parents' house in Berkeley, where I lived during college. We had an off and on-again story long distance through our teenage years. She would later convert to Judaism and was already circling around the idea, whereas I, having attained the age of reason back at the time of my bar-mitzvah, had concluded I didn't actually believe in any of the stuff I'd been taught by the religion professionals. We may well ask whether an adolescent might be anywhere near the age of reason, but in the fifty years since I can confirm that my mind and heart have never had regrets about that early understanding. Nonetheless, I remained curious about spiritual and mystical questions, and about the music and literature and history and culture of Jews in their migrations worldwide. So, one day Judy posed the perennial question: What makes you Jewish if you're not going to go to *shul*, and celebrate *shabbos*, and do all the other practices? I hardly had the language to articulate an answer, with its million and one reasons or a succinct summation thereof, and with my eyes wide I simply blurted out, Everything! Religion was the least of it, I tried to explain, not quite getting through.

A large part of my childhood rebellion against religious studies was not a mere rejection of authority—that was easy, that was natural—but rather the *absolute* authority that insists this is how the world is, like it or not this is reality, these are your forefathers, this is how you came to be from ancient times, these are your sufferings, this is what you must do. I could not accept that the whole big song and dance laid out before me was my world, no ifs ands or buts: this is your life and welcome to the family. Really? That's all? Even at a young age I could see there were lots of things—lots of people—who did not fit into that picture. So, instinctively I always objected to the arrogant pricks of my own religious background who would pretend their show and tell of piousness made them holier than thou, because they were living how we (who?) were supposed to. When I take a drive, turn right at the corner on Bedford and a few miles up the road pass through south Williamsburg, and I see all the Hasids like out of 18th-century Ukraine, it gives me the willies. My wife can't stand the way they dress and the rampant sexism of the men, but she's not Jewish, it's worse. They're a little bit closer to me. I've known of them all my life, like that could be me had I taken a horribly wrong turn. Would that they were all just wise old storytellers out of Martin Buber. Fundamentalists of all stripes I find annoying as can be, but this is another order of magnitude. Quite instinctively, I have always looked upon such Hasids, in rare instances of proximity, as at creatures in a zoo, only to realize with a shudder that they could be my distant cousins.

One facet of Jewish style that I appreciated even as a child in Torah studies was the instinct for commentary. Was Rashi more legal scholar or literary critic? That love of discussion, of argument sometimes, seemed a mark of being alive, of grappling with the world—when it didn't descend into cheap tactics of manipulation. All depends on the spirit of inquiry. I might have almost been taken in, therefore, on my infrequent encounters with another sect of Hasidim, the only proselytizers among Jews, the Chabad-Lubavitchers. They like to talk. They engage with people, and are likely to be warm and welcoming. But they have a purpose in their outreach, to gather in those who strayed, those who might harbor a secret yearning to come home, as some see it though I don't. First of all, I didn't stray. And then, I was not about to be roped in by god hustlers no matter how nicely they talked, because I didn't buy what they were selling. You'd see them on streets and corners in Brooklyn in the fall: pasty-faced, malnourished young men in their standard black hat and suit, open shirt, one of the two holding the *esrog* (citron) and *lulav* (palm frond) as they approached a passing stranger. "Are you Jewish?" If the response was even hesitantly affirmative, they beseeched you to join them in the blessings for the holiday of Sukkot, handing you the *esrog* and *lulav* to shake on cue, while repeating the Hebrew words as recited. I remembered those items from childhood, so out of amusement I went along with their routine the first time they came up to me, decades ago. But right after, though I had accepted their bit, I sort of felt used. Each fall they'd be on the streets again, like starlings eager for pickings, and I soon grew hostile to their approach. One day, a few years back, my buddy Kip arrived to housesit while we were away. He went out to his car to retrieve more bags, and since he'd been out there a moment I went to see if I could help. There, standing beside him by the open trunk, were two young Lubavitchers deep in conversation. Kip's mother was Jewish but he hadn't been raised in the religious or mystical elements, only the Marxism, from his grandfather. Once I saw them, I knew it best for me to go inside, no point standing there just looking hostile. Never, Kip said when he came in, had he seen my face change like that from bright to dark.

My discomforts with the religion I was born to are hardly uncommon. I've known people who envied the ritual practices I grew up with; they had nothing to reject in that way. Perhaps my grown children will feel the same some day, deprived of obligatory religious rituals through their childhood—but they don't yet.

Worn to Wonder

How do we not realize, day after day as we reach into our closet, that clothes are the ghosts we once wore. We are not jealous that they will outlast us; we give it no thought at all. And why would we, for that "once" denotes a past that hasn't settled into place yet. As we glance about our shelves, our hand grazing over the hangers, we let our mood or purpose on that morning inform us what to lift down upon our empty arms. Some private joy maybe, a secret message, a whisper of hope tucked into the fabric carries us through the coming hours; we can only trust they will still be there to make us visible by the end of the day. However much consideration we may spend on them, our clothes remain articles of faith, projections of our presence in the outside world. They might be merely a uniform, identical to a thousand like it, except how we wear them, how we move in them, beyond our conscious intentions, describes something of the person inside, something that is solely ours. The clothes wear us, it would seem, animated by the spirit we bring to them.

That spirit, with its particular dreams and sorrows, its accident of time and place and person, leaves a trace in those threads that may not ever be known or identified.

Nonetheless, we recognize an unspoken dialogue waiting to engage us, if only we linger and listen. How to draw it out, how to understand its form of testimony. In their Saturday Profile the other day, the *New York Times* focused on Julia Brennan, whom the writer described as a "textile conservator" (Zoey Poll, "Preserving Brutal Histories, One Garment at a Time," Jan. 23, 2021). She might well be called a detective, diviner, clothing whisperer. Though museums and collectors have indeed asked her to preserve historical items—Abe Lincoln's greatcoat the night of his assassination, Babe Ruth's kimono—she has in recent years improvised new methods to treat and analyze clothes left over from mass atrocities: a Khmer Rouge prison, the Rwandan genocide. Faced with more than a task of conservation, she invested the imagination and sensitivity to question these garments, alert to small details. Through the generalized trauma and the crud of oblivion, patiently she was able to glimpse something of the lives that inhabited individual pieces of clothing. As if a measure of the light hidden in them might yet be unlocked, she let the material itself tell her who had been there.

Standing before the array of our own wardrobe, we see precious little of the days and years folded into such tactile archives. A few fleeting memories perhaps, a partial catalogue of tastes and whims. And how many items pushed to the sides, not quite abandoned, escape our notice, near strangers to our existence now? They might still fit, who knows, if we contort our way into them, and what then—all fantasy shed in an instant, our tenuous connections back to them broken by the changes we embody. We cannot be surprised to find our closets turned into a museum at the edges, where forgetfulness and denial would also cover us before the evidence is pushed out the door, lovingly or with indifference it doesn't matter. We hesitate to get rid of our old threads because vaguely they remind us of a certain continuity, relics of our folly that evoke a complicit fondness, as if we know better at this late date. That shirt, what were we thinking? Those shoes, where did we imagine we would wear them? In a struggle for space, or moving house which thereby precipitates decisive actions, we jettison the items that have lost all shred of meaning, sober eyed for once.

Our old clothes, the ones that hang about among our shelves as in a waystation of oblivion, in choosing to cut them loose finally we allow that spirit which we lent them to roam free of us as well. It might suit someone else a while. That accounting is not for us to reckon. The garments that remain stubbornly in our care, though they may go untouched for years, when death comes knocking, violently or with the gentlest kiss, that is when they most belong to us. Text and textile become as one. Our words, our thoughts, our loves, our tears, woven through time into the cloth that embraced us over and over again, for however long, cast a resonance that others may hear on a lucky wind, when least expected.

What Do People Do in a Garden State

Though I don't recall any of my own teachers laying on me the damning advice, for decades after it seemed the mantra of most writing teachers across the United States: Write about what you know. Not that the perspective is wrong so much as misleading and simplistic, befitting the reactionary times in which it held sway. I grew up in suburbia, through my early teenage years, and if there was anything I certainly did not want to write about, it was suburbia. I did not want to read about suburbia either. Its familiarity, its comforts, its safety all seemed deadening, and once you woke up from it there was no going back. The Jersey shore was a particular kind of suburbia, initially of late nineteenth-early twentieth century vintage, but the effect was the same. Why would anyone want to leave if they did not have to for work or family circumstances?

Having left before an age where the choice was fully my own, I discovered another outlook. Almost anyone who knows me has heard me declare: New Jersey is a place to come from, not to go to. I mean, I do understand the attraction for anyone who is not from there, a lot of beautiful spots throughout the state, and much more pleasant than the constant challenge of wrangling with an overcrowded, expensive metropolis. Often I have thought that, despite its small size, New Jersey is rather a microcosm of the entire country. But most people I have known or read about who are from there, happen to live somewhere else. Coincidence? Typical American migration? This is not to suggest the triumph of the Empire State with its towering ambitions. We're all the same shmucks wherever we live, though the where does condition the how and who we may become. I would never deny that I am from New Jersey, and I even take a perverse amusement from that fact, but at a distance. Whenever I go there, to visit my mother-in-law in the western part of the state or down to the shore where I came from, my internal clock starts counting the hours. A night or two, no problem, and good morning to you, only soon a sort of primal dread wells up in me that I might not ever escape again.

Who knows, life with its cosmic tricks and inscrutable ironies may determine that I spend my final days in New Jersey, however I do not intend to help along such a twist. Or I could find myself in some anonymous suburb across another state line, what's the difference. And yet, I have always wondered, a little, about those who did not leave, for whom the thought or desire to go live elsewhere, at least to try and see what that might be like, did not materialize as a real temptation. Probably most everyone they knew, family and friends, remained in the vicinity, so why make trouble for yourself? Or was it a lack of curiosity, of need, of possibilities? I might well ask the same, of course, about people in California or any other region. Is New Jersey a state of mind? Americans generally know of it as a punchline, at minimum, but what exactly is the joke? And why do so many of us recognize a personal imperative to get out before it's too late?

One could live quite comfortably there, no doubt. Nothing to disturb your routine, in normal times. The stuffy, chaotic big city beyond the horizon counts for little more in the end than a shopping trip, a bite of entertainment. That is the wonder of suburbs: they're nearly self-contained, an archipelago of similar places joined by local roads. If you mistake one for another, you'll get used to it. And what's most equal of all in suburbs is the boredom.

I know I'm being unfair, but maybe not. The *je ne sais quoi* of New Jersey that so many take pride in (might as well) is instead, or simultaneously, a *je ne sais que trop* for the rest of us natives. Anything can be interesting, no matter how mundane, within limits. The open secret about what you think you know, whether family or place or longtime habit, is once you look into it, poke around inside a while, it turns out to be full of a lot more than you signed up for. That might be beneficial or not for the writer seeking to write about what they know. On the other hand, some teachers challenge that very assumption: Write about what you *don't* know. Because there, we discover enormous room for play, and in fact we likely know far more than we thought. Tales of suburbia, common as they may be, draw us in most where they focus on what does not fit: the kids or adults who are desperate to get out, who just could not fit if they tried; or, considering most aren't going anywhere, those who are riddled with colorful eccentricities, thereby at least internally carving out a distinct space for themselves. It is not only the big city that poses challenges for survival.

So, is New Jersey a state of merry (or grumpy) misfits? Hardly; wouldn't that make it a fun place to visit? What it has, on an elemental level, is the capacity to remind us that no matter how grand your pretensions or renown, regardless of your achievements or how much you've traveled the world, you're still from New Jersey. You can make it in New York all you want, be the toast of the town or a star in Hollywood—you are still from New Jersey. That means some form of cozy suburbia probably nurtured you, for better or worse, or some small city that exhausted its potential long ago were it not for new immigrants, places that told you go on, beat it, there's nothing here for you. For once, maybe you listened. But to those who remained, who found satisfaction enough in what life offered there, your departures were just seeds in the wind, not their concern. A thought, a memory, carried away past the next row of hedges, and the next after that. Weeding, trimming, that's what people do. Things keep growing back, they'll make a mess of the place if left to go wild.

Finders Keepers

Purity arguments inevitably seem unconvincing to me. Social Register primates, aristocrats, Jews, African Americans, whoever else, all have their reasons for keeping the mating dance an in-house affair. If not purity, then preservation of wealth, culture, something called identity. Heavens to Betsy (who is Betsy and what have we done with her?) that you should wander outside the circle. Gnashing of teeth, rituals of mourning, there goes another. That is called adventure, to reach beyond the group; can't last, not supposed to.

Before we married, my wife had been friends with an older Jewish couple; once I came into the picture, I would go along to visit them. The man died and we continued to see the widow occasionally. When my wife announced we were going to be wed, the woman was happy for her but lamented that I, the Jewish one in the pair, was marrying outside the faith. Her friend, my bride-to-be, was inadvertently enabling one more to elude his duty to perpetuate—something.

Whoever's job it was to drill that into my head, the sense of duty so defined, must have gotten distracted or recognized the odds. Somehow, I could not manage to find myself a *nice Jewish girl*. Not that I tried. Would that mean vacations in Florida? No thank you. An endless series of ritual gatherings forever more, the extended family sporting their pedigrees in business and medicine and law? Wasn't exactly on my radar. I mean, I did have a Jewish girlfriend here and there, nothing serious. My main college romance was a girl whose mother had taken her off to Beverly Hills in her early teens, from halfway across the country, so they wanted to think they might be Jewish further back in the maternal line, the cloudy German origins. It's true I didn't help matters, with my bohemian ways, jeopardizing my own potential as a nice Jewish boy. The whole scenario seemed too predictable, swallow me up like Jonah's whale and away we go. No, instead when I got involved with a Jewish woman, more than I bargained for, I had to go all the way.

Seven or eight months in Paris, I went to a party out in the near suburb of St. Cloud, invited by three women journalists I had met at a press event weeks earlier. Two were American and the hostess Canadian, all freelancers like me, in our mid-twenties. Whatever reticence I may have had in going, I was caught off guard by the wiry, fast-talking woman who answered the door and was apparently those days sleeping on the hostess's couch. As the evening wore on, I kept coming back to my conversation with the woman, who seemed quite different from the rest, with her caustic humor, her cigarette breaks, her unnamed urgency. Because of her I stayed until midnight, and so, despite vague words of caution from one of the others, I saw her again. Quickly enough, I learned from her that she was the daughter of concentration camp survivors, that she was eight years older than me and born in Poland, that it was all she could do to break away at last from her parents and Montreal, and that no sooner did she arrive in Paris, she tore up her return ticket and threw it in the Seine. I'd never met someone like her!

How do you spell trouble? Let me count the ways. I was too young to settle down for life, but she had no time to waste, not when her very survival, let alone that rare bloom called love, were threatened at every turn. She was indeed uniquely intelligent and equipped with the sensitivity to appreciate the most unadorned instances of beauty and poetry, while having no patience for bullshit, intellectual or otherwise. As I got more and more involved with her over the next three years, I wondered how I was ever going to extricate myself. Her whole existence seemed to be constantly hanging by a thread, and it was in my hands whether she sank or swam. I wasn't eager for that much responsibility. Finally, I announced that it had to end, which took another six months to materialize when she found herself a studio a few blocks away. What part inertia, resignation, fear, what part shared pleasures, even love? I wanted my life back, whatever that meant.

Though their story might well be as simple as it appears, I have never heard of possible romances in the past of either of my parents before they met. Were they, in effect, pre-programmed to marry someone Jewish like themselves? In America, as children of immigrants, that would seem a likely prospect, though hardly a done deal. Trauma, menace, solidarity, such experiences bind a community, reinforce the imperative to stay together, even to believe in their own myths. Of my parents' generation, I think all siblings and cousins married within the fold; of my own, about half. If one finds cause to worry about those tendencies, the evidence is there, for what it's worth. And funny thing, in my own generation the ones who kept to the ancient directive betray a certain pride, as if to claim a pure allegiance.

Families and tribal groups carry their particular self-protection mechanisms, but the light can get awfully dim inside. There is a comfort, a reassurance, in sticking with your own kind, like you don't have to explain anything. Is that not an illusion, though, like purity itself? Those of us who refused to listen, to countenance the supposed limits of bloodlines or ancestral promises, our small rebellions were just a way of seeking clarity. To let the unsaid, unseen, unheard take us down its bright paths, where we might find our own true home.

Like all bad dreams, this seemed quite real. And yet, it could only happen through unconsciousness. We first rolled into Oaxaca hours earlier, where we found a hotel without much trouble—one of those affairs with an elaborate inner patio garden, and the rooms off the corridors beyond. We put our bags in our rooms and headed back out to see the city while we still had half the afternoon. Someone suggested the steam baths, which sounded like a good idea, to relax and freshen up after driving for hours to get there. Isaac or Nicky procured a joint from the proprietor of the baths, even better. And so, we shvitzed and got stoned a while, and when we were done wandered over to the central market area nearby. We plunged in among the different stalls, so much to look at. Before long, I got separated from the others, and glancing about I saw that I was suddenly on my own.

Having never been to Oaxaca before, I realized I was completely lost. Could I even find my way back to the hotel? From that street to the steam baths to the market area, we had taken enough turns that I no longer felt too sure which direction it was in. No use to panic, that could come later. I just had to keep walking and enjoy myself, take my time there. You don't think to notice every detail, entering a new place, as if you were stepping into a labyrinth. It doesn't occur to you how easily you might lose track of the people you came with, and what then. I was bound to run into my friends eventually. Of course, I would.

The situation grew prolonged, however. So much casting an eye out for a familiar face was getting tiresome. What was I going to do? How would I explain? I wasn't a little kid; although I was not entirely grown up yet either, if that mattered. No plan of action was taking shape in my mind. Maybe if I stopped strolling around for a spell, let the crowds pass by. My friends might emerge when least expected. But how do you catch the unexpected by surprise? And then something else caught my ear instead. A young woman standing at the counter of her stall was singing a tune, wordlessly, that I recognized. It was not a Mexican tune. From across the world like a signal it had landed there, by some unfathomable route, and I stumbled forth from my own great distance to hear it. Only a few years earlier had I heard that song for the first time, on a record I found at the Berkeley Public Library, or maybe a cheap used copy chanced upon at Moe's Books: Pete Seeger and Frank Hamilton's *Nonesuch and Other Folk Tunes*, on Folkways. An old Russian song, "Meadowland," the melody had stuck in my head—as it has to this day, fifty years later. There seemed something miraculous about us meeting like that, me, the song, through the woman who was not much older than me, but I did not let on. I lingered just close enough to listen and yet remain unnoticed, to not disturb her brief reverie and mine as well.

CANARY

We may not really be there, wherever *there* is, not in the flesh and blood, but more than ever now in the digital age we can be practically anywhere we want. In spirit, in thought, in the resonances pulsing through our nerves. Is music enough to transport us, when there is no memory or frame of reference to anchor the sounds? Somehow that does not seem to matter. We do not have to love Jesus, or want anything to do with him, or have the slightest grounding in the language that praises him, to be stirred by Jesus-loving music, by qualities of the song, the lament, the hymn, by the raw voice, the raw instruments, that carry the yearning. Or, to cast in quite a different direction, the music might brandish neither identifiable purpose or source, might defy stylistic definitions or recognizable forms, and yet it could still take us places—mysterious, unsettling, or confoundingly sublime. But there is also the vast submerged continent of lost times, vanished places and people, that the history of recorded sound—only since the late nineteenth century—hauls to the surface. What started mostly as commercial products, for the specific context of earlier generations, through the evolution of technology become archival documents, at a shimmering remove from all of us.

Some record labels devote a portion of their catalogue to rescuing such documents from oblivion. Frémeaux et Associés, near Paris, has tapped a rich vein in state archives and other sources well beyond copyright limitations to reissue many box sets not just of early twentieth century French music but also of foreign styles, performed both in Paris and on their home terrain: tango, gypsy, fado, chôro, beguine, and various forms of jazz. These vintage recordings command attention, challenging the listener to reimagine a settled past. Canary Records, a label out of Baltimore and keeping mostly to a digital existence, has focused primarily on music from eastern Mediterranean immigrants recorded in the United States long ago. Or as founder, producer, researcher, and clear-eyed obsessive Ian Nagoski describes his ongoing project of the past decade: "early twentieth-century masterpieces (mostly) in languages other than English." One could listen at random to any of the several dozen compilations and hear plenty of heartache, just in the tonalities and having no sense of the words, but also small moments of joy and promise. We could imagine the music reflecting the immigrants' travails as no doubt it does, though such projections soon become blurred by the very nature of melodic practice in those cultures of origin, which favored minor keys and modal structures. Nonetheless, the voices do sometimes convey their own cry of anguish mixed with grace, some eastern Mediterranean form of divine inspiration. We hear it; we want to hear more, yet we know as well that we must not hear too much.

The pungency of the titles of many releases on the Canary label gives a good indication of what lies in store for us. *No News from Tomorrow: Greek and Turkish Speaking Jewish Women in New York. Send Me the Bones: From the Earliest Syrian-American Recordings. I Was Born a Badass Chick: Greek Music in NYC in the 1940s-50s.* Other immigrant communities are also granted a renewed presence thanks to Nagoski's inveterate crate digging. *The Dull Hatchet: Late 1940s Lemko Instrumentals in Brooklyn. You Are the Light of the World: Antiochian Byzantine Hymnody in Toledo, Ohio.* These are worlds that most listeners, including me, know practically nothing about. Even their descendants probably retain little connection to the fading remnants. The music surfaces again as more than so many curiosities, from somewhere beyond the bubble of nostalgia or a nagging dream, almost familiar, stubbornly out of reach. We are the outsiders on listening, due not only to language and the distance of time, but to that concept of home posed by the music. A provisional, imagined, declarative, emotional home, somewhere between the old world that is no longer and where they find themselves in current circumstances. The descendants themselves might have a window onto that place, though not much more. This too is part of the great panoply of American roots music, but uprooted, the original soil still clinging to the exposed roots.

Canary—like the canary in the coal mine? Or, like that bright little creature in its lonesome cage singing its heart out? Surely both and more, harbinger of our disaster but also of our continued escape. If only we lend an ear. Even so, there's no guarantee we will always be lucky. America is a land haunted, from top to bottom, by the dispossessed. Each immigrant is a gift of hope and gratitude, while it lasts, still to this day. If our ship appears to be sinking, our burdens and disarray too overwhelming, that cannot be laid at the feet of those just arriving. The immigrant music of a hundred years ago, or eighty or seventy, brought to our door by Canary, though intended for particular communities in their time, hangs like a lantern in the dark night to remind us that life finds a way, if we choose to honor life and remain unafraid.

A Feather Blows Us Over

You might well be in your right mind, your right body too, yet you got up on the wrong foot and the whole livelong day tumbled forth as if its nuts and bolts were barely hanging on. Just one push, at the right moment, and it could all come clattering down. Somewhere near the start you got distracted, an unfinished thought, your simple morning habits tripped out of order to set your rhythm askew: you reached for jam before you thought of butter, locked the door behind you without your wallet, walked down a different block and promptly forgot where you were going.

How easily we fall from the grace of unthinking, our automatic pilot jolted to attention, which flounders amid shuffled points of reference. It is not that our routines are so complicated, but we each have our way of doing things, how we were taught and how we adapted those practices, mix in a few odd twists, so that the merest blockage can be enough to knock us for a loop and suddenly we're improvising. With recent pains making it difficult to bend my arm in back of me, I started slipping my left arm first through the sleeve but when the right kept jabbing about in search of the arm hole, it was like I'd forgotten how to put on a coat, what are the mechanics. Here I was in a slapstick comedy, I could not get out the door. Moving along down the street after that, I wondered about the people I saw around me, what unexpected obstacles had they overcome to appear so normal and unremarkable?

Or I go to the gym, the locker in the corner that I usually head toward is occupied, which causes me to lay out my things elsewhere, not along the windowsill as I like. Though I'm certain I have what I need, something seems missing and it's not until halfway up to the pool that I notice my feet are bare, did I not see the flip-flops in my bag, but pressed for time I continue on my way, alert now for puddles by the poolside. That is where bacteria spread and I have come down with plantar warts more than once, it's not fun. Conscious of my bare feet gripping the stone floor differently, I'm careful not to trip from thinking too much about them.

The marvel about that sort of glitch is it catches us off guard every time. Without fail, the thing that's nudging us to skip a beat is so negligible, not worth the mention; we're hardly able to explain it. But its effects ripple through the day and we keep refining our adjustments. Maybe it is a luxury in the first place, even to have a rhythm that one could be thrown off. No doubt everyone has their rhythm, which we don't have to think about until we do. When there's a disruption, or we look up to see a tree standing before our path, so we step aside, go around it. I could imagine those disruptions are really the norm anyway, and who among us gets to follow their own rhythm from start to finish of a single day? And how would we know? We're too busy working and trying to work. A feather blows us over, we wonder where it came from.

Propelled by a Stranger
to Unexpected Delights

The particulars are hardly extraordinary on their own. Because Rene's birthday was coming up soon, I wanted at least to get her the new Jackson Browne record, since she has remained a fan of his music throughout his long career. The great omnivore Amazon, with its sinful convenience, let me down for once: first, they said shipping would somehow take a month, then they were out of stock altogether. That wouldn't do at all. But there are no record stores anymore! Online I found a small shop in San Diego that had it, then I hesitated, what with shipping cross-country. Surely there must be somewhere in Brooklyn that had it as well. At last, I found a place with the plainest name, Compact Disc Shoppe, way out on Avenue U in Sheepshead Bay, a four-mile drive south along Bedford Avenue. Not wanting my prolonged effort to be drawn out further, I set off within the hour, heading across town on a Friday afternoon.

The store was small, and most of the records seemed to be used, though I saw no clear arrangement in the layout of the shelves. The owner, behind the counter, was talking up the new George Harrison reissue with another old-timer as they groused about kids these days. I wondered how any store like this manages to survive anymore. After the drive, of course, I had to look around a bit, but was glad not to find much that I had to have. Any moment I was going to ask for the title I requested by phone that he set aside, except then I started glancing through a set of shelves by the door. The bottom five racks were all classical, a fair amount twentieth century, and on some high-quality labels. He told me those records were all a dollar per disc, part of an estate sale he'd bought recently, a bargain, of some eight hundred classical titles. Before long, I was putting more money on the parking meter and looking through two of the four boxes in the back room, as I amassed a stack of possibilities that got whittled down to fifteen. Along with the three items I'd found for the birthday gift (two of them new), pleased with my adventure, I had to get out of there.

Here is where the stranger enters. The entire ride home, I couldn't believe my luck, what a trove. And at that ridiculous price! Each time I stopped at a traffic light, I would peek over to the sprawl of CDs in the passenger seat, looking to composers and titles to remind myself how many times a sort of lightning struck. Messiaen,

Ligeti, Ives, Poulenc, Busoni, even my contemporary Kaija Saariaho, the Finnish composer. Who was this person, I began to wonder, to have built up such a collection? Clearly someone with discerning taste and a substantial knowledge of the Western (and Northern) classical tradition. There were plenty of other titles among the several hundred I perused that either I had or had heard, besides the robust array of opera and vocal sets that didn't interest me but would have made a maven weep from embarrassment at the riches. And who was the broker or friend who had engineered that sale of the deceased person's impressive music library? Why to Randy the owner of the Compact Disc Shoppe? Was Sheepshead Bay the common ground for all of them? Pardon my assumptions but I had not imagined such a sophisticate in that neighborhood. Did the person have friends there too who shared these passions?

Through the weekend I listened to several of my new acquisitions and continued to marvel at the bounty I'd hauled in. I thought of the ones that got away, left behind, titles that caught my eye but I didn't take time to investigate. And what of the two boxes I didn't look through? Several hundred more, gathered by the same curator. I understood this was not the same as simply shopping by composer, say, among currently available releases. For three-plus decades, someone was carefully making those selections that I got to choose from. I realized I trusted that person's eye. By Monday morning, I was thinking it might be worthwhile to drive back out there, take another look at what I'd missed. I owed that to my unknown friend. I was bound to turn up more treasures. They should just find a good home, was the broker's comment to the shop owner.

In the back room of the shop, I pulled up a chair and moved the boxes around, the better to dig through them. Randy was working at his desk there on his secondary business, or maybe it was primary, insurance. I didn't ask what kind of insurance. Slowly, from the boxes, I extracted another stack of CDs while the door announced just two visitors: a customer he knew, a woman in her sixties picking up DVDs, and an oldish man in awful shape who took two steps inside, declared he was sick, and requested an ambulance be called. Apparently, he had asked at other businesses on the block. Randy hastily said he would but implored him to wait outside, which the man did, sat on the sidewalk right next to the door. The ambulance arrived promptly, and eventually so did the tuna sandwich ordered for lunch an hour earlier. I went out and put another half-hour on the meter, finished up in the back, and looked through the shelves by the door again. In the end, an even dozen was my tally this time—Elliott Carter, Ruth Crawford Seeger, *Schoenberg in Hollywood* (photo of the middle-aged Viennese composer in pink short-sleeve shirt and white khaki pants playing outdoor table tennis). Berio, Nono, Cowell, Varèse. Also, a curious anomaly: Jack Smith's *Les Evening Gowns Damnées*, readings and performances from 1962-64. This person, whoever they were, what did their home look like, their furnishings? And if Jack Smith figured in the collection, did that suggest a touch of outrageousness in their personal style, something that set them apart from their neighbors?

Could be he was a longtime music teacher at one of the public high schools in the area. But that would be sad to think not just that he died alone, but none of his former students were close enough, or deserving or interested enough, to inherit such prizes from him. Maybe he wasn't a music teacher, but rather a postman. I thought it likely this person was a man. Did he inherit his late mother's house? The music was like his private garden. He must have listened often. In any case, he had flown the coop by the time I stumbled in there.

It's not that I dislike vocal music. But sitting at my desk, I do not usually want to be listening to voices or words, especially in languages I understand. If it's part of a predominantly non-vocal record, fine, depending on who's involved; certain modern composers, I'll make exceptions. In those two dozen records I selected, there were so many moments of discovery as I listened over the following days and weeks—composers I knew, a little or a lot, but mostly not those specific works—I tried to parcel them out to last longer, the experience of first hearing each one. There was a double-disc release I was looking forward to, from my second visit, small ensemble pieces by Christian Wolff, *(Re):Making Music, Works 1962-99*, played by The Barton Workshop. He's a composer I didn't know well but I wanted to hear more. I was enjoying the delicately jeweled pieces, spare yet enormously expressive, and before I knew a woman was singing. Entering under cover of a cello and a clarinet and a wandering whistled melody, she sang a piece called "A woman invented fire." I'm often wary of musical settings of poetic texts, but I rather liked this one, so that was a nice surprise. In too many instances, composers drown the poetry, the music in the words, but here they were given room to breathe. The woman's voice was left to lift and float on its own, the instruments dropping out to let her go. Then I found that the poet was Grace Paley, the marvelous writer of short stories but whose poetry I had thought slight when I read some years ago. I saw, in the booklet, there were eight of her poems set to music, and as I read them and heard the voice that embodied them, I thought they are not slight at all, they are just right, full of love and compassion, humor and wisdom. I would not have had the chance to appreciate them, to be surprised by them, had I not made the journey to Avenue U.

Rooms

If there was a name to the restaurant, I didn't see it. Down on Kingsley Street, one block over parallel to the beach, the locale was hardly distinctive: just another prewar apartment building. The area was familiar enough—Palace Amusements at the end of the street with Tillie's grinning face painted on the wall and the dizzying funhouse inside, the boardwalk along Ocean Avenue where I liked to play miniature golf, even Asbury Lanes on a side street back when it was simply a bowling alley. But this place I wouldn't have known until my parents found it. I must have been about eight or nine, and catching sight of the small sign hanging from the fire escape over the doorway, I announced what seemed to be the name of the establishment, "Rooms."

But to say establishment is to lend an air of permanence, which was hardly the case. As I recall, the restaurant stayed in business for only one summer, maybe two, not off-season. I did express the desire to go back to eat at Rooms, so I'm sure we returned. My hundred-year-old mother remembers the place was one flight up, the walls painted blue, and the décor quite unadorned. What left more of an impression, it was the first time I'd heard of

Armenians. Who were these people? To judge by their food, they were all right by me. Most important, though, I discovered lahmajan there, the small individual pizza with minced meat and vegetables. In all the decades since, I have remained on the lookout for that savory appetizer, and found it under different flags, with slightly different spellings and pronunciations. But tasting it each time, I recognized it as the same.

The Way of the Dodo

You have to have lived enough in the twentieth century to appreciate not what they are, or were, but their centrality in the smooth functioning of society. Practically every resident in any town large or small had one of these doorstops, even several, and the distinction of white pages as opposed to yellow pages persists to this day. Granted, that difference doesn't matter in the application of its secondary function in delivering a good beating and leaving no trace, but a wooly nineteenth-century type of novel, or an unholy Bible, or a dusty and longwinded scientific treatise may serve almost as well; except that the pages were larger, thus a bigger wallop. With so many names and lines of small print packed in there, it offered more information per square inch of paper real estate than anything else. Kids who've come along since, what can they know of the glories of the phonebook, that humbly democratic institution which embraced nearly everyone?

Automatic bestsellers, irrespective of region or demographics or education, they were not so much read as consulted. More or less reliable, trusted, they helped establish the existence of each person who lived in a place. There on paper, it says so. This is you, your address, your phone number; or those were your details. But technologies change, the world of humankind splits again and again in the way it does things. The phonebook is weightless now, immaterial, ever incomplete, and often confusing. We might find anyone, if we're lucky, or at least a distant trace, though we may have to search along many paths and through multiple lives joined only by that name across a great expanse. When it was still a book and not yet an electronic resource, when it still had body, there was just one edition in an area, published by the local phone company. With constant harvesting of the most basic facts—where a person can or could be found—we appear dispersed, strewn across innumerable fields. If we ever did, we no longer live in one place. What seemed evidence of our whereabouts echoes mutely, erratically.

Surely not all copies of the print versions have been pulped, even at this late date. As creatures from another era, they no longer fit anywhere, their use superseded. If it were a work of imagination, of crazy faith, of scientific rigor, there might be a cult or fetish value. But a directory of names and their coordinates in a given year? Nothing is gained studying such raw data, except possibly in the eyes of a social researcher out for a joy ride. Who would collect these books, organize them in a museum, a library, a curiosity shop? As object, reflection of an epoch or style, its presence has faded completely from our lives. Where it still surfaces is to suggest that place as well may fast be vanishing—or already lost, unreachable. Phonebooks on a special shelf, hanging against the wall, piled on a table, we knew where they were kept. To chance on one today, forlorn, can only be disturbing: a thing that makes no sense in the current ordering of our systems. Even if the names in those pages are still breathing, and at the listed address, not many people answer landlines anymore!

Another few decades, the transition will be fully achieved. The surviving phonebooks can be lifted proudly from their cluttered corners, charged with a new purpose. Housing an entire city of the dead, it names each person who once walked among us, or before us. When we call their number, and no one seems to answer, it will be because we are not equipped to hear them.

Homing Instincts

Every one of us in our own world who each had our relationship to the place but we the swimmers at the Eastern Athletic pool in Grand Army Plaza, within a matter of days, suddenly after so many years hit a wall. The new landlords were draining the old pool because of insurance issues, they claimed. No indication of eventual reopening, and so just like that, before we could believe what was happening, everyone was there for their last swim. In the notice posted on mirrors and partitions, the wording did not say explicitly that the pool was shutting down for good, but that's how we all took it to mean. In any case, the end or whatever it was happened in a flash. No time to linger over that view from the seventh-floor poolside windows. Barely a few moments to prolong conversations with other regulars, none of whom did I know well beyond countless brief dialogues. Yet here we were with empty arms, caught short as we realized we might not ever see any of these people again; except, possibly, in the neighborhood or else migrating among other pools.

The move fell like a bomb in the midst of all our intricately spun rhythms day to day. That pool was indispensable, a regular destination for hundreds of us. Many, especially older members, might not recover from the toll of less convenient alternatives, considering that most people walked there. Having no pool could in turn cause a decline in body and mind, for those who had the habit—let alone its effect on the people losing their jobs, notably Erick, head lifeguard for the past 24 years who taught our kids how to swim. Suspicions were that this business was a real estate ploy, some kind of maneuver to maximize their assets. Empty the building, then major renovations and sell off as condos. Mysterious machinations. Surely the change of ownership was not mucking things up? On the other hand, finances were not so peachy before that, as longtimers were aware. The problem lay in multiple directions, from mismanagement to conniving to more mismanagement.

What we knew about any of this now or in the past, concerning the history and administration of our pool, was the product of those fleeting dialogues, a mulch of facts found and imagined, along with observation, speculation, interpretation. Mostly, no one thought about it too much, they came and went, happy for a swim—until it wasn't there anymore. Our knowledge, such as it was, was really a collective product: all those people we'd spoken with through the years, in the elevator, at the front desk, in the locker room, by the pool. Not that we retained a lot of that second-hand information, but generally we had a sense of how things operated; any persistent dysfunction was due to the age of the building, which the owners never sufficiently dealt with, from what we had seen. One only had to take the elevator a few times to get a sense of what that meant.

On the other hand: such were the partial accounts we gathered that it was easy in the rush of events (from the users' standpoint, since we learned just three days before the pool closed) to forget the possible negligence of the health club. After all, the pool had leaked—and in the first year of Covid, expensively flooded the floors below— several times on their watch. Who was responsible for the pool we swam in year after year, the owner or the tenant? And were not we, the swimmers, the ones most put out by the failures of all responsible parties? We who were more familiar to each other than strangers, yet not friends either for the most part, members of a reluctant tribe. In our solitary sport none of us sought solidarity, but the water conferred it.

So, what was going on here? That remained the ongoing question a week later. I saw two separate notices to their respective constituents, first from the health club and later Garfield Temple (the current owner, located ten blocks away, who took over this summer from Union Temple, the original owner), essentially blaming each other for having to drain the pool. Whoever bears ultimate responsibility, the situation is a mess. The lawyers and bankers can bicker, but the swimmers will move on. Just six days after my last swim at our old pool, I signed up for membership at a brand-new community center in Crown Heights, reconverted from a hundred-year-old armory, that's closer to my house. And exceedingly cheap since I now qualify as a senior. Limited hours in the morning for lap swimming, which was the deal-breaker for my wife who found it first, but they suit me. When I visited at that time, in the six lanes there were only two swimmers floating back and forth, strangers still to me.

A day later, I returned for my first swim there and it was exquisite in the nearly empty pool, no one in the lanes to either side of me beneath the high windows and arched ceiling of the former armory. The whole facility had been open barely two weeks, so I should expect to see more people eventually. Until then, I will enjoy the great luxury of having the pool almost to myself. Already in the locker room I confirmed that the fellow I'd spotted way over on the other side swimming leisurely was indeed Boris, the gentleman I knew from the old pool. And on my next swim, I saw that the Orthodox woman had returned, whom I had passed down the block without recognizing her as she rounded the corner. It was clear from my initial visit, walking a different route—up Bedford and across Empire, past the Ebbets Field apartment block, past Medgar Evers College and on up nearly to Eastern Parkway—that we were in a neighborhood distinct from the previous place though just blocks away. Whatever reluctant tribe might form by way of the pool, unbeknownst to us, at the Major R. Owens Health and Wellness Community Center, I was glad to be part of it from the beginning. Given the early hours of lap swimming, I might not ever glimpse the full extent of young and old to dip, struggle, or delight in that same water, but our voices were let loose there, our breath, our wild and soaring thoughts.

Jason Weiss was born and raised at the Jersey shore, schooled in Berkeley, spent a decade in Paris, and has been living in Brooklyn for 30+ years, working as a writer, editor, and translator. His first book was *Writing at Risk: Interviews in Paris with Uncommon Writers* (1991), followed by books on Brion Gysin, Steve Lacy, Latin American writers in Paris, and the ESP-Disk' record label. He also published *Cloud Therapy* (2015), short nonfiction texts on swimming, and translated books by Luisa Futoransky, Marcel Cohen, and Silvina Ocampo. With Iris Cushing, he co-edited a big book of selected poems by the late California poet Mary Norbert Korte (1934-2022), *Jumping into the American River* (2023). Spuyten Duyvil previously published another book of short nonfiction texts, *Listenings* (2023).

www.ingramcontent.com/pod-product-compliance
Lightning Source LLC
Chambersburg PA
CBHW011236120626
46549CB00009B/3294